"In this inviting text, based on sound principals of developmental psychology and clinical experience, the authors have accomplished making the often-dreaded task of anger management in children easier, even playful. I highly recommend this practical guide to parents, teachers, counselors, and their young charges."

—Susanne M. Jensen, Ph.D., clinical psychologist, Baton Rouge LA

"The contents of this workbook reveal that we are never too old to learn how to manage our own anger, as well as that of others. This workbook should prove to be a valuable resource for parents, teachers, school psychologists, and other mental-health workers."

—Alesia M. Williams, Ph.D., school psychologist, New Orleans, LA

D1395766

Helping Your Angry Child

Worksheets, fun puzzles, and engaging games to help you communicate better

Darlyne Gaynor Nemeth, Ph.D. • Kelly Paulk Ray, Ph.D.
Máydel Morín Schexnayder, MS

NEW HARBINGER PUBLICATIONS, INC.

Publisher's Note

Distributed in the U.S.A. by Publishers Group West; in Canada by Raincoast Books; in Great Britain by Hi Marketing, Ltd.; in South Africa by Real Books, Ltd.; in Australia by Boobook; and in New Zealand by Tandem Press.

Copyright © 2003 by Darlyne Gaynor Nemeth, Kelly Paulk Ray, and Maydel Morin Schexnayder
New Harbinger Publications, Inc.
5674 Shattuck Avenue
Oakland, CA 94609

Dialogue Guide in chapter 11 is used by permission of the author.

Cover design by Salmon Studios
Text design by Michele Waters

ISBN 1-57224-312-0 Paperback

Printed in the United States of America

New Harbinger Publications' Web site address: www.newharbinger.com

05   04   03

10   9   8   7   6   5   4   3   2   1

First printing

This book is dedicated to our parents who created wonderful RILEE Families: Marie and Benjamin Gaynor, Derra and Hershal Paulk, and Sonia and Manuel Morin.

Contents

PART II
Good Teaching: The First Four Steps

PART III
Good Relating: The Next Four Steps

Acknowledgments

This workbook is the product of almost a decade of work in the area of anger management with children. It first began with clinical interventions for brain damaged children who had difficulty with basic facial discrimination. Feelings such as fear, anger, anxiety, embarrassment, sadness, and happiness were very difficult for these children to discern.

In our work with many different types of children in many different settings, we came across the same information. Whether these children had emotional, behavioral, learning, adjustment, or brain problems, the results were the same. It became apparent to us that all children, even normal children, need to learn how to recognize, label, and share these six basic feelings in order to have positive interactive experiences. The feeling that was most problematic for children to learn to display correctly, however, was anger.

We began to develop intervention programs that were appropriate for different children in family, school, and social settings. Due to our belief that learning how to manage anger appropriately is necessary before children go through puberty, we have concentrated on elementary school children. Our Let's Talk About Anger program has been used in school settings with great success. We've presented it at numerous conferences, including the American Psychological Association's annual meeting in Washington, D.C. in the year 2000. Now, due to the diligent persistence of Jueli Gastwirth at New Harbinger, our work has evolved into this workbook. It is our hope that this book will help parents, teachers, and counselors to assist children in dealing with their most intense feelings, especially their feelings of anger, more effectively. This is, indeed, the key to success in life.

We wish to acknowledge the following individuals and interventions sites for their significant contributions to the evolution of our program in anger management training for children:

Tracy S. Hopkins and Michelle D. Barquero (psychology externs from Southeastern Louisiana University); John Brun, Ph.D., Alan Taylor, Ph.D., Linda Upton, Ph.D., and Mark Zimmerman, Ph.D. (members of the Psychology Consulting Committee at CPC Meadow Wood Hospital); C. Christiane Creveling, MA, Christine Mangus, MS, Nina S.

Broyles, LCSW, JD, and Joni Wiliamson (group facilitators and presenters); the Neuropsychology Center of Louisiana, LLC, the Drusilla Clinic, and Meadow Wood Hospital in Baton Rouge, Louisiana, and Donaldsonville Elementary School in Donaldsonville, Louisiana. A special acknowledgement is offered to Warrine Lightfoot (parent activities coordinator) who introduced our program to Donaldsonville Elementary School.

We also wish to acknowledge the unceasing support of our loving husbands, Donald Nemeth, Richard Ray, and Edgar Schexnayder, who were most encouraging RILEE Bears. Additional encouraging RILEE Bears include Madeline Nemeth, daughter of Darlyne and Donald Nemeth; Richard Gaynor, brother of Darlyne Nemeth; Alexander Ray, son of Kelly and Richard Ray; and Angela Boudet and Migdalia Perez, grandmothers of Maydel Schexnayder. We also wish to acknowledge the artistic contributions of Monica Schexnayder, who brought RILEE Bear to life. This workbook would not have been possible without the tireless efforts of Keri Walters who helped format and guide its development from the first stage to the final stage. Hers was indeed a major contribution. Another significant contribution was made by Sarah Savoy, whose research skills were commendable.

An editor of extraordinary caliber was needed to help the authors be consistent in their presentation. Dr. Annette McCormick, retired professor of English at Louisiana State University, rose to the occasion. The authors are grateful to have such a wonderful mentor and friend.

Introduction

You are about to begin one of the most important journeys of your life. It is a journey that you and your family will complete together. It is a journey of loving family relatedness, which is essential for managing intense feelings, especially anger. This workbook offers a road map to help you along the way.

Being a good parent is one of the most important tasks in life, but few people are really prepared for the challenge. This book is for parents of angry children and for parents who want to learn how to be better parents, in order to avoid having an angry child. It is also for young parents, parents with young children, or parents who are interested in learning more about healthy emotional expression and creating a loving family environment. We believe that creating a more loving family environment is the best way to help your angry child. When families feel free to discuss their emotions, negative feelings do not intensify and are easier to manage. Remember, anger begins with you. In addition, counselors and teachers can use this workbook, since they often deal with angry children.

It is our belief that, to be successful, children must learn to manage their anger before puberty, as this is the time when children tend to act out rather than talk out their anger. Therefore, we concentrate here on elementary school–age children.

The workbook is divided into three parts. Part I covers what good parenting is all about. It gives you an opportunity to recognize and resolve any excess emotional baggage that you may be unknowingly bringing with you on your journey. It helps you to get rid of any that have accumulated from your past. Most important, it prepares you to become the loving parent that you have always dreamed of becoming.

Becoming. What a wonderful word. It invites growth and change. It encourages learning and caring. It is about being true and being real.

The process of becoming a good parent requires all of this and more. You can do it. Armed with the perspective you will receive from part I, you will be prepared to face one of the most difficult emotional challenges of family life—dealing with anger.

Part II offers you four chapters on ways to recognize, label, and deal with this very powerful feeling. Anger can interfere with everything and everyone. It can ruin your dream of creating a loving family. With the knowledge and tools presented in this part of the workbook, you will become an effective teacher.

Part III completes the process by showing you how to address and resolve this intense emotion within your family structure. By avoiding getting stuck in unresolved issues and mastering effective ways of relating, you and your family can continue on your journey of love.

We believe that:

> Love is about commitment.
> Commitment is about responsibility.
> Responsibility is about freedom.
> Freedom is about rights.
> Rights are about choices.
> Choices are about judgment.
> Judgment is about maturity.
> Maturity is about being real.

And when you have become real, you can give the gift of love.

Part I: Good Parenting: Be Prepared

In chapter 1, you will learn new ways of relating to enhance your parenting skills. Families come in all varieties now. In the past a typical family included mother, father, sister, and brother. That is now an atypical, rather than typical, family structure. Now, families include a mother and children, a father and children, two mothers and children, two fathers and children, grandparents and children, and all sorts of other combinations. Relating is learned in the family structure, whatever that structure is! This workbook teaches the RILEE method of family life. It is about *relating in love every evening*, for that is when the family can take time to relate. This relationship model can then extend to school, work, and community life. For the purposes of this workbook, all guardians or primary caretakers in a child's life will be referred to as *parents*.

In chapter 2, you will have an opportunity to examine family affective themes, or what we call FATs. These are the historical emotional tone in one's family which is often passed on from one generation to another. Today, there is no good, bad, right, or wrong family. There is only your family. The goal is to learn to relate effectively. This workbook will facilitate that learning. You carry emotional baggage from your past family to your present family. You need to have an understanding of the emotional baggage that you carry and perhaps some of the hurtful experiences that have weighed you down. You and your family will be asked to explore old and new concepts and ideas. You need to address and eliminate your FATs. This must be done through "exercise" and "diet." In this chapter the exercise is about sharing your thoughts and feelings, and the diet is about changing your behavior.

In chapter 3, the six types of FATs are explained. Please note that this chapter is for adults with baggage. In this chapter, you will have the opportunity to explore the six most common family affective themes: fear, anger, anxiety, embarrassment, sadness, and happiness.

The healthy family has all of these feelings, in perspective. No one feeling is dominant. Therefore, when you are with this family all feelings are acceptable, as long as the behavior is appropriate.

Chapter 4 is a sharing experience for all family members. It is an opportunity to put the six basic FATs in perspective so that no one family affective theme dominates; therefore, when you are within your family, all feelings are acceptable, as long as they are expressed properly. Anger is the most problematic feeling to express properly. Some families hold anger in and never resolve it. Other families let their anger out and create more problems. Healthy emotional expression resolves problems.

Part II: Good Teaching: The First Four Steps

In chapter 5, you will learn more about the relationship between your thoughts, feelings, and behaviors, as each "feed off" of the other. Specifically, you perceive an event, have a thought about it, then feel something specific about your thought, which ultimately leads to a behavioral choice. What contributes to your perception of events? Whether you realize it or not, everything you do involves a choice. Sometimes the choice you make is based on allowing old family affective themes to overwhelm you.

Usually, you might be able to "balance" your strong emotions within your families. On occasion, however, when your family's expression of emotions becomes too strong, a disruption within the family occurs. If this happens too often, relationship problems arise. For most families, the expression of anger is usually the focus of these problems.

In chapter 6, you will learn why anger is so powerful. Unfortunately, the problem with anger is that it works in the short run. It is an effective stopper. It is a good weapon. It makes us feel very powerful. But you have to be out of control to achieve these successes, and you hurt others in the process. In the long run, you hurt yourself and your relationships. Eventually, you end up alone. Therefore, acting on anger is not okay. By teasing, blaming, wanting too much, and challenging others, you stay on the angry path and never reach the RILEE path.

In chapter 7, you will learn how to identify the many facets of anger. Simply stated, anger is a feeling. It is how your body responds when something happens to you that is unpleasant. When you get angry, your heart beats faster, your temperature goes up, and you may start to sweat or become flushed in the face. We discuss how wallowing, intruding, circular thinking, and overreacting keep you from the RILEE path to relating.

In chapter 8, you will learn how to manage this powerful feeling. Controlling anger means that whenever you get angry, you will let your family know about it in a way that keeps you from getting hurt or hurting others. When you control your anger, you are taking charge. You must learn to be the boss of your emotional expressions. It's easier to do this when you *know* that anger is a choice.

It is important to promote empathy in your family. Sometimes you have to look past the anger to see the real feelings.

Part III: Good Relating:
The Second Four Steps

In chapter 9, you will discover the key to relatedness. There are different ways to let family members know when you are angry. Here the family will learn three types of voices (passive, aggressive, and assertive) that will help you identify which voice you use and which voice will be more effective for you. Everyone needs to practice healthy emotional expression.

In chapter 10, alternatives to anger will be explained. Whenever your children feel angry, it is important for them to find healthy ways to feel better. Often, just helping your children reduce the stress they feel can help them to understand what is going on inside of them. Practicing attachment parenting will help you relate to your child and identify their feelings. In this chapter, you and your family will learn several ways to reduce tension and feel better. Deep breathing, relaxation, choosing your battles, using code words to help each other remain in control, and giving each other time-outs are all healthy choices.

In chapter 11, you will have an opportunity to develop new ways to talk out old and new hurts. Learning how to share your thoughts and feelings and learning how to actively listen will be the focus of this chapter. For example, when you use open-ended questions with your children, you encourage communication. You can also help your children to be more aware of the way they speak and the social cues they give and receive. Helping your children to become effective communicators is important.

Lastly, chapter 12 brings the eight steps of parts II and III and the perspective of part I together. It will remind you that all members of your family need to be in charge of how they feel. Your family members need to be considerate and caring, yet free to express their own individuality, through thoughts, feelings, and behaviors that work for them. The key is for you and your family to express yourselves in a way that honors and respects each other. Being out of control is not okay. When your family is connected in a RILEE way, you have eliminated the FATs.

Note: This workbook contains a lot of exercises to do with the family. Please photocopy them as necessary so that everyone may participate. You will notice that some of the games are geared to capture the interest of young children. All family members, however, are encouraged to participate.

PART I

Good Parenting:
Be Prepared

Are you prepared to be a good parent? Did you learn good parenting skills in school? Did you learn good parenting skills at home? If the answer to any of these questions is "No" or "I'm not sure," this workbook is for you.

In Part I you will discover a new approach that will make parenting a little easier. This approach will include more effective coping strategies, behaving in a friendlier manner, and understanding yourself. You will also develop an awareness of the emotional baggage that you bring to the task of parenting. You will be given an understanding of the developmental and emotional issues that can interfere with effective parenting. And you will learn how to create a healthy family. With RILEE, or *relating in love every evening,* parenting can be a joy rather than a burden.

chapter 1

A New Perspective

Learning new ways of relating can enhance your parenting skills. Having more effective coping strategies can improve the quality of your family life. Behaving in a friendlier manner toward those who love you can make a difference. But you have to be different to make a difference. Making a difference is about understanding yourself. This requires a new approach.

In today's busy world, it is easy to simply stay frozen in the "here and now." Don't look back for perspective. Don't plan for the future. Just stay in the present. These are common messages in our society. But they are too shortsighted. You need your past to be grounded. You need your present to be challenged. And you need your future to be uplifted. It's all about understanding the roots of your past, the reality of your present, and the wings of your future. Wings are about dreams. Dreams are about finishing unfinished business and inviting the impossible to become possible. And the reality of the present is about coping and letting go.

It's the letting go that is the most difficult task of the present. Oftentimes, you know what needs to be done and perhaps even how to cope with the situation. But letting go of your feelings is hard to do. Without taking time to resolve your feelings, you simply store them. Then these feelings become a part of your past and interfere with your future. The most difficult feeling to let go of in the present is anger, yet relating depends on effective anger management.

Be Prepared

Are you prepared to be an effective anger manager? Do you end up holding onto feelings deep inside of you, or do you believe in letting it all hang out? When you let your anger out, do you do so in a hurtful or respectful way? Good parenting involves using warm and responsive words and/or gestures toward children to shape their behavioral development. Unfortunately, it is too easy to slip into bad parenting. Perhaps there was a time when you used angry and reactive words and/or gestures with your children. Perhaps your parents used those same words and/or gestures with you. Perhaps your children will use those same words and/or gestures in their lives. Or, perhaps not! It all depends on you. One thing you can do is relate in a loving way.

Respectful families relate in love every evening. You might say, why in the evening? Well, family life has undergone radical changes. Most families do not even eat breakfast together anymore. Now, morning is about getting up, getting dressed, and getting going. There is no time for relating, only for getting going. This workbook teaches the RILEE method of family life, because the evening is when families can take time to relate—if they choose. If *you* choose. In an atmosphere of relating, it is possible to be a good parent.

The Impact of Anger

Anger—what a powerful feeling! Yet it is clearly the most destructive of all human emotions. As you read this book, it is important to have a clear understanding of anger. Anger is a powerful negative expression of rage, which may be displayed in words and/or gestures ranging from mild displeasure to overt hostility. It significantly interferes with relating. In fact, when anger begins, relating ends. These two forces cannot exist in harmony.

The need to relate is basic. Children are born with the need to attach (Bowlby 1969). They are not born with the need to express anger. Distress, yes. Anger, no. So where do children learn to be so angry? Most likely in their family structure. (Note: By *family structure*, we mean people living and relating together in the same household who may or may not be genetically linked.)

Early Learning

How do children learn to be so angry? Most likely, by imitating the adults in their family structure. The primary method of early learning is imitation (Gruber and Voneche 1977). Children imitate what they see, what they hear, and what they experience. They typically do not do what they are told to do. Rather, they do what they are shown to do. Most parents do not realize the powerful ripple effect that their own behavior has on their children's learning and memory.

Gender Differences

It is also important to realize that gender plays a part in children's early learning experiences. Sadker and Sadker (1994) point to the early success that girls experience in schools, whereas boys seem to have a harder time catching on to the requirements of the educational system. They suggest gender bias on the part of the reinforcers (the teachers and parents). It is possible that gender bias exists, even in the most nurturing educational systems. Another explanation for this phenomenon, however, is the gender difference in the early learning process.

In our work, we find that boys tend to learn primarily from experience rather than from example, whereas girls can learn from either example or experience. Thus, it is not uncommon for a young boy to be told "Don't touch that plate. It is hot." The young boy will typically touch the plate and respond, "Ouch, it is hot." A young girl will typically say, "I'm not touching that hot plate." This ability to learn from example is very helpful to young girls. Both boys and girls, however, do benefit from experience. Thus, this workbook is designed to teach through experience and example.

The Impact of Relating

Relating is a positive, meaningful exchange involving words and/or gestures. It is inter-active and requires clear, concise commands and/or statements. Relating respects the need for clarification of both the message and the expectation. It is important that you teach your children how to relate. Here are some tools.

Avoid No's, Nots, and Don'ts

A child might have difficulty restraining himself or herself from touching a hot plate because of the way in which a command has been stated. Clinical experience with Thomas Budzynski's pink noise biofeedback device, the Twilight Learner, revealed that people typically have difficulty understanding commands that include negatives such as no's, nots, and don'ts (1977). The command that was given in the above example was, "Don't touch that plate. It is hot." It is typical of a parent telling a child what not to do. But this negative command is less effective than stating what you want your child to do.

Use Positive Commands

Children respond better to positive commands. "Use an oven mitt to pick up the plate" is a much clearer command than "Don't touch the plate. It is hot." The positive command includes only one concise sentence. It also provides the child with a distracting command. Thus, it is easier for the child to respond in an obedient manner. The child knows what to do, rather than what not to do. There is less confusion. There is also less chance of the child being hurt.

Be Aware of Your Power

Remember that you as the parent and teacher are the rewarding agent. Children want to please you and be rewarded by you; a *reward* is a positive or wanted action given to encourage behavior. Children want to love you and to be loved by you. Oftentimes, they just simply do not know how to accomplish this task.

Setting children up to succeed in relating is your primary job. Children cannot be expected to somehow figure this out on their own. They need help. You can use positive words and/or gestures that will assist your child to get on the RILEE path. Here are some examples of *helper phrases* that you can use to help your child please you and love you:

* ✳ "I like when you give me hugs."

* ✳ "Mary, you are doing that so well."

* ✳ "Johnny, that's a really good question."

* ✳ "You can do this."

* ✳ "Keep up the good work."

* ✳ "I can see that you are figuring it out."

* ✳ "Your drawing is wonderful."

* ✳ "You used so many beautiful colors."

Find the IQ-EQ Balance

Oftentimes parents are so concerned about developing their child's cognitive intelligence or intelligence quotient (IQ) that they overlook the need to develop their child's emotional intelligence or emotional quotient (EQ) (Shapiro 1997). *Cognitive intelligence* is a person's ability to learn, understand, and use mental knowledge to think, plan, solve problems, and behave effectively. *Emotional intelligence* is a person's ability to learn, understand, and use affective knowledge in order to sense and feel emotions and behave appropriately. It is not uncommon for children at all levels of the IQ spectrum to have deficient emotional intelligence. Children need a balance of the two in order to learn. You can help them find this balance by rewarding both their IQ and their EQ efforts. Using phrases like these will help them to find this balance:

IQ Helpers

"Mary, you figured that out so quickly."

"Johnny, you thought before you acted."

"I like when you show me how many words you know."

"Gee, you really know your math facts."

EQ Helpers

"Johnny, thank you for considering Mary's feelings."

"Mary, it was good that you made room for Johnny."

"Thank you for sensing how tired I was."

"I appreciate that you shared your popcorn with your sister."

Understand the Goal of Child Rearing

It is not uncommon for parents to see in their children opportunities to fulfill their lost wishes and dreams. As a parent, you might want your children to make the football team or cheerleading squad that you didn't make, to go to the school that didn't accept you, to play the violin that you could never master. It is very easy to see your child as a little person who can fulfill your dreams and expectations. But child rearing is not about cloning. It is about growing. You have a responsibility to your children—and to society—to teach them to be who they can be and to help them to live in a world that they can shape. Children must learn from you how to be themselves, not how to be you. This is one of the most difficult tasks of child rearing. It requires unselfishness and altruism. Understand the goal. It's not about you. It's about them. Thus, learning to be a self-sufficient, caring, productive adult who contributes to family and community and who understands the balance between work, family, and play is the goal of child rearing. This requires relating!

Feelings and Facial Expressions

It is essential for children to learn to recognize and understand their own and others' feelings, or emotions. A feeling is not a thought. Often, children become confused because they have difficulty correctly perceiving the facial expressions of others, especially their parents (Dodge, et al. 1984). Have you taught your children to recognize the feelings on your face?

Have you taught your children to discriminate and label these feelings by looking at your face? Do your children get confused by what you say versus what they see? One explanation is that they may not have been taught to discriminate among the six most common feelings: they cannot tell the difference between scared, angry, anxious, embarrassed, sad, or happy looks on your face. Oftentimes, parents expect this just to happen.

In part II of this workbook, there will be several exercises that will help you make sure that you and your children are recognizing and perceiving each other's feelings correctly.

Know the FAT

Sometimes family affective themes, or FATs, may interfere with a child's ability to correctly perceive the facial expressions of others. We define FATs as the historical emotional tones in your family that are passed on from one generation to another. This topic will be covered in greater detail in chapter 2. For now, just note that everybody is going to have to deal with their FATs in order to relate properly.

Catch the Double Bind Messages

At times children receive *double bind* messages. This is when you thwart your child's coping ability by giving two contradictory messages at the same time (Guerin and Chabot 1997). The two messages could be "You are smart; you are dumb." The second message may be sent in either obvious or subtle ways, and while parents are usually unaware that they are giving double bind messages, the results are nonetheless damaging. For example, you might unknowingly say, "I am very unhappy with your behavior," while smiling at your child. Such messages must be caught and replaced with noncontradictory messages.

Nonverbal expressions are usually far more powerful than verbal expressions. In the example above, smiling is a more powerful message than the verbal statement. The child heard that you were unhappy with her behavior, yet she saw you smile. Children who are parented through double-binding messages often become confused and anxious. They cannot figure out what you mean or how to please you. The following double bind box will help to illustrate this point.

Everything in this box below is true:

```
Mom is unhappy
(verbal statement).

Mom is happy
(gesture).
```

Figure 1.1 The Double Bind Box

The most important idea here is that everything in the double bind box is true. You can see how confusing this is for children.

Eliminate the Double Bind Box

When children are given double bind messages, they feel boxed in. The double bind box is a very dangerous place for children. It confuses them and thwarts their development. Often, children act out to get out of the double bind box. One common form of acting out is active defiance. A child, therefore, might respond to your smiling face and verbal statement, "I was very unhappy with your behavior," with an angry emphatic, "I don't care!" Yet children really do care. Perhaps children display an air of angry contempt because they do not know *how* to please. Seldom do parents realize that their ineffective methods of relating (double binds, confusing commands) cause their children's angry reactions. In most cases, when children are getting it right and becoming effective at relating, it is because their parents are effective communicators.

Create a Safe Emotional Environment

Relating, or communicating, is a two-way street. Parents often expect to be heard without affording their children the same privilege. Being heard is essential to avoid being hurt. Children must have the opportunity to respectfully clarify any confusing statements or commands. In this regard, active listening is an essential part of relating.

Use Active Listening

Active listening involves four components: listening attentively and completely; summarizing what you heard the other person say; restating the agreed upon summary; and finally responding rather than reacting. Sometimes having your child simply restate the command eliminates many interactive problems. This exercise is offered to illustrate the active listening process.

Exercise 1.1 Active Listening

1. Johnny comes to you and tells you that he didn't make the soccer team because his grades weren't high enough. What do you say? Check off the statement that would most accurately describe your response.

_____ "Johnny, you didn't make the soccer team because your grades weren't good enough?"

_____ "That coach was looking for a reason to dump you."

_____ "What is wrong with you?"

The first response tells Johnny that you have listened attentively and summarized what you heard him say. With the other two statements, you are either blaming the coach or saying something that is damaging to your child's self-esteem.

2. Which of these three statements would be your next response?

_____ "That's awful."

_____ "How do you feel?"

_____ "So you didn't make the team because your grades were too low?"

If you chose number three, you have restated the agreed-upon summary. Then it's time to respond.

3. Which of these three statements would be your next response?

_____ "You are so dumb."

_____ "Johnny, I'm so sorry. Have you thought about ways to bring up your grades?"

_____ "I'm going to get that coach fired."

If you chose number two, you have acknowledged Johnny's information and frustration with support and concern. Any other choice just fuels the fire and furthers the hurt.

Sometimes, when your child approaches you with something important, however, you might not really attend to his or her words. This happens to all parents. When this happens, just simply say, "I'm sorry. I wasn't paying attention. Would you please repeat that?" Children are good at giving parents a second chance. Be good at giving them a second and a third and a fourth chance, or as many chances as they need.

Build Mutual Respect

The essential element of mutual respect must be present if relating is to be successful. You need to be courteous and polite to each other. As a parent, you expect respect from your children. But do you give them respect? If respect is not given, how can children learn to give respect? Remember, children learn through imitation.

Eliminate the Stoppers

Given a busy work world in which rudeness rather than respect often dominates, it is very easy for parents to return home after many hours of work totally exhausted. If you work outside the home, you may be on "emotional empty" when you reenter the home environment. Perhaps you may be a stay-at-home parent who is looking for relief at the end of the day. You may have very little to give. Yet the emotional demands of the home environment are ever present.

Often, to escape these demands, you might use angry expressions, stoppers. *Stoppers* are negative words and/or gestures that prevent a person from getting on the RILEE path. In the short run, these angry expressions do work. They stop the process. But at what cost! Usually, children are eager to see the parent who has just come home from work. They are merely trying to connect, to relate. Yet they are punished for their efforts. When you use the following stopper phrases, you are punishing your children for trying to connect:

* "Leave me alone."

* "Can't you see I'm tired?"

* "Just do it."

* "Because I said so."

* "I just sat down."

* "You always want something."

* "Don't bother me."

* "Ask your dad/mom to help you."

When you are too tired to relate, you may use anger as a temporary stopper. Though this may work for you at that moment, it can be damaging for your child in the long run.

Give Yourself a Time-out

A *time-out* is an intervention technique which can be useful. If your children are not able or willing to relate or behave appropriately, you can remove them to a quiet place, which allows them to calm down. One minute per year of age, not to exceed fifteen minutes, is the recommended amount of time (Hall and Hall 1987). This technique can also be used for adolescents and adults. You can also give yourself a time-out, and doing so can be a more appropriate intervention than always putting your child on time-out. Time-outs must be used consistently and for the same purpose across the board, but they should not be used because you need a break from the demands of relating. When you are out of control, call a fifteen-minute time-out for mommy or daddy to calm down.

Teaching children to respect family members' boundaries can be an essential part of relating. For example, when you take "Mommy time" or "Daddy time," your children learn through imitation to have "kiddie time." In each case, the time taken is a short break from the family for rest, or peace. Mutual respect increases when family members can recognize when they need a break. Everyone, however, will need practice doing so in a responsible way. Do you remember the little boy who cried wolf so many times that, when the wolf actually came, no one believed him? He lost his credibility. It is important to be able to honestly communicate your needs.

Know When Enough Is Enough

In an ideal world, it would be wonderful if you could meet your child's needs at all times. In the real world, however, the ability to meet someone else's needs is finite, not infinite. Thus, one relating concept children must learn early on is that of *satiation*, or knowing when enough is enough. For example, in regard to satiation, a child needs to be taught that one scoop of ice cream is enough, or that one hour of play after school before beginning homework is enough. Children need to understand limits, the point at which their behavior can no longer be tolerated by another. But likewise, so do parents. Often too much is expected of children: they must make all A's and be on the soccer team and play a musical instrument and be popular.

This concept of satiation is important to the development of your child's self-esteem. As much as you need to express your love for your child, you need to teach your child that he or she can't have everything. Children need to develop a sense that there are reasonable limits; without a sense of limits and boundaries, children don't feel secure.

Keep the Past in the Past

Parents sometimes try to work through unresolved childhood issues by putting additional burdens for success on their children's shoulders. Children often fall under the weight of such pressures and either turn their anger inward in passive depression or turn their anger outward in active defiance. By the time this has occurred, a child's self-esteem has already been deeply wounded. Children cannot carry the problems of the past on their shoulders. Just dealing with the problems of the present is enough of a challenge. Children do not need a double layer of responsibility.

Use Rain Checks

One technique for teaching family responsibility is a *rain check*, an agreement to deal with something at a later time. This is a wonderful family technique for teaching responsibility. For example, your child wants to go to the movies, but you cannot afford the ticket. You might request a rain check and offer to take him or her to the same movie, at the same time, at the same price in two weeks. Then, in two weeks, you must follow through.

Without keeping your word, there is no credibility, and this form of relating will fail. It is also important if you take rain checks to allow your child to use them too. That is, if you tell your daughter to put out the garbage, she can say, "I am on the phone. I'll take a rain check. I will put out the garbage in fifteen minutes." When fifteen minutes have passed, she has to take out the garbage, or she will lose credibility.

Restructure an Unsafe Emotional Environment

Without credibility, a family does not function very well. When you cannot count on each other, the bond of trust is broken. Thus, it is hard to maintain a safe and loving family unit. An angry family structure emerges.

Family Paths

All families have a path to travel. The path toward real love—the RILEE path—is outlined in figure 1.2. If the coin were flipped, however, that same family would be on quite a different path—the angry path.

RILEE path = polite and courteous behavior → respect → trust → comfort → love.

Angry path = rude and abusive behavior → disrespect → distrust → distress → hate.

Figure 1.2 Family Paths

Practice the Six RILEE A's

Healthy families practice the six RILEE A's. They give each other attachment security, attention, acceptance, approval, acknowledgment, and affection on a daily basis. In this loving RILEE environment, self-esteem, mutual respect, satiation, proper limits, and rain checks come together with good emotional management to form a very functional family unit.

Unfortunately, families too often focus on problems, or on those times when they are dysfunctional. The spotlight is usually on the dysfunction or the reaction. The old saying "The squeaky wheel gets the grease" certainly applies here. Bad behavior is noticed and reprimanded, whereas good behavior often goes unnoticed and unrewarded. When children are angry or wild, they get noticed. Thus, children come to a point of dysfunction because of how they are noticed and reprimanded, not because they are innately bad. The flip side of the relationship coin looks like this: lack of bonding, negative attention, rejection, disapproval, disregard, and frustration. When these are a parent's practices, children will react accordingly. That is, bad behavior produces bad behavior. (See figure 1.3.) Many children grow up in this type of family environment, only to later take their anger into their school and community.

The RILEE Side

1. Attachment security
2. Attention (positive)
3. Acceptance
4. Approval
5. Acknowledgment
6. Affection

The Angry Side

1. Lack of bonding
2. Negative attention
3. Rejection
4. Disapproval
5. Disregard
6. Frustration

Figure 1.3 The Relationship Coin

The Essentials of Good Parenting

Remember, children want to get it right. They want to succeed in pleasing their parents. You must figure out healthy ways to let your child succeed at the most important task in life, the task of relating.

This workbook addresses the task of relating. It gives you the essential tools and techniques you need to teach your child the important elements of relating. As stated earlier, children must be taught relating skills. They are not born with them. They are not born with anger either. Both are learned. Typically, both are learned at home through imitation.

Let yourself succeed. By addressing your unstated family affective themes, by offering acceptance of the child you have, rather than continuing to long for the ideal child, by giving up unfulfilled personal dreams and expectations, by looking for ways to reward what your child is doing right, or almost right, by letting your child succeed at a realistic level, and by equipping your child with the tools and techniques of relating, you will be able to approach your goal.

Find the Right Balance

It is easy to put work above parenting. But these important adult responsibilities need not be mutually exclusive. Again, you should try to achieve a good balance of work, love, and play. Healthy parents know how to create this balance in their own lives and how to apply it in their parenting. Good parenting is a lot of work. Active teaching is required.

Parenting requires a great deal of love. Loving your child means accepting your child as is. This type of unconditional love, which was first conceptualized by Carl Rogers (1959), is a basic human need. Without it, frustration emerges. Chronic frustration often leads to rage, which is difficult to soothe.

Yet play can be a welcomed pressure release. Play reduces defensiveness and increases closeness. It helps families have fun together. Play often breaches angry feelings, thus allowing relating to emerge once again (Jernberg 1979). This workbook offers many experiential play activities, designed for this purpose.

Respect Your Children's Strengths and Vulnerabilities

It is important not to take advantage of your child's vulnerability. When your child takes a risk to trust, that trust must be maintained.

It is also important to respect each other's strengths. In this workbook, you will be able to teach your children to be assertive, to keep themselves calm in the face of difficulty, to develop a true awareness of their own and other's feelings, to listen, to be heard, to be understanding, and to respond appropriately. These tools will equip them with very powerful relationship skills. But these tools are not "sometimes" tools! They are tools for all times and all situations. On some occasions, you may not want your children to be quite so effective. But you cannot pick and choose. Honesty, insight, mutual respect, self-esteem, trust, and vulnerability are all parts of relatedness. Discretion, of course, is also part of the relating process. Censorship is not.

This workbook is designed to help you help your children express all feelings—not just some feelings—but appropriately. Appropriately—that is the key! Anger is perhaps the hardest feeling to express appropriately. What do we mean by "appropriately"? In this context, appropriately is defined as being done in a way both people (you and your child) can handle. You must let your child know acceptable times and ways to express feelings, especially anger. Likewise, this process must be mutual. Children must be allowed to be assertive and effective in the home environment. What they learn at home they will use the rest of their lives.

Bring Others Up to Date

Children often behave as either weak or wild. Either position is an unhealthy coping strategy. Children also go through phases, and if your child is going through a weak or wild phase, you may need to introduce your child's new behaviors to other important family members. Communication is especially important between divorced or separated parents when a child is living in more than one home. It is also easy for grandparents, teachers, and other caretakers to mistake weak or wild relating techniques for signs of disrespect. For some adults, any change in behavior on a child's part is interpreted negatively. Thus, children who are in the process of change must be protected from those who do not understand what is going on. Often, all that is needed is communication among the adults. In situations where this may be difficult to accomplish, written notes may be helpful. Most teachers will be happy to schedule conferences to discuss these issues.

It should be a comfort to know that the tools and techniques offered in this workbook have been used in varying forms in clinical, hospital, and educational settings. They work! They reduce anger and disruptive behavior. They increase relatedness and harmonious behavior. Children can learn to be more effective communicators. Children can learn how to be more assertive regarding their own needs, as well as how to be more responsive to the needs of those around them, whether it be the family, a team, a class, a club, or a gathering of friends.

Learning Is the Purpose

The purpose of this workbook is to learn. In this regard, it is important to remember how people, young and old, learn and develop memory traces. A *memory trace* is the automatic storage of bits of information in your brain from past experiences to help with future expectations. We learn in two ways: Through *incidental learning*, we acquire knowledge or skill accidentally and effortlessly. *Intentional learning*, on the other hand, requires purpose and effort. According to Betty Fielding (1999) four processes are involved in intentional learning: visual, motor, auditory, and thought. You can help your children learn and remember a new concept or behavior by using positive words and gestures—what we call *helpers*—and by avoiding negative words and gestures—what we call *stoppers*.

Helpers (What to Practice)

1. Calling your child by name

2. Touching your child

3. Looking at your child

4. Giving one positive auditory command/statement

5. Asking your child to repeat the command/statement aloud

6. Asking your child to practice the required/expected behavior

7. Reinforcing your child for getting it right or almost right

Stoppers (What to Avoid)

1. Overteaching

2. Using negative gestures

3. Using double bind messages

4. Giving multiple commands

5. Making confusing statements

6. Shaming

7. Scolding

In closing, we want to reiterate our belief that when children know what to do and how to succeed at doing it, they will do it; especially when the rewards are present and the FATs are resolved. You can now begin your new journey by beginning to understand your emotional baggage. Remember, any unresolved emotions and issues that you bring to the parenting table reduce the chances of a successful RILEE outcome for your child. By understanding yourself, you can be more effective at relating. This is true for both you and your children. Best wishes for a meaningful journey. We truly hope that you and your children will choose the RILEE path.

chapter 2

The Old Baggage

The purpose of this chapter is to help you deal with the emotional baggage in your family. This is important because all baggage gets heavy when carried too long. Thus, the contents of your baggage need to be examined regularly. Afterward, you will have the opportunity to make better choices about what is best for you and your family to carry or to discard. Lightening your load is always a good idea. We've included some fun activities to further illustrate the main concepts here.

Your Emotional Baggage

What is emotional baggage? A feeling (for example, being anxious) is an expression of your current affective state. It is not a thought! An emotion refers to your ongoing mood state, which is made up of several different feelings. An emotional state occurs when your body reacts to your experience of strong feelings. Remember the definition of anger from chapter 1? *Anger is a conscious feeling, based on the aroused state of rage, which is an emotion.* Emotions often have a physical component (i.e., you may blush when you are too stressed), whereas the feeling of anxiety is usually caused by the worrisome thoughts that you are thinking. How does that fit in with emotional baggage? *Emotional baggage consists of negative feelings that preoccupy you and that you carry in your memory traces over an extended period of time.* You experience emotions and carry those experiences with you everywhere you go. But how do you get them?

Emotional Traces

Your body remembers emotions. A trace of emotional pain, for example, is felt, even when no memory exists to explain it. Therefore, you tend to repeat your mistakes. Bar-Levav (1988) believes that feelings and emotions are passing reaction states, or temporary responses to the current situation, and not excuses for irresponsible behavior. Deep seated emotions exist in everyone, though not everyone recognizes current feelings. According to Bar-Levav, culture plays a role in this. For example, Western culture dictates that you must numb yourself against your deep-seated emotions. You tend, therefore, to react to situations with strong feelings, but you are not often aware of the feelings you are experiencing that are causing your reaction. Learning how to deal effectively with your emotions is the first step toward enjoying the present.

Family Scripts

Another way of "getting your emotional baggage" arises from your family. *Family scripts* contain identifiable traditions and expectations for your family that are transmitted from generation to generation (James and Jongeward 1973). In other words, your family script is made up of those historical traditions and expectations that limit your ability to choose a new path. Parents usually expect their children to carry on these traditions. This is one example of "inheriting" emotional baggage.

If a child chooses to follow an alternate route, rather than to carry on the family script, that child may become the family "outcast." A child may choose an alternate route as a result of counseling or some other type of individual intervention. For whatever reason, the results, though in the family member's best interest, may disrupt familial relationships, thereby causing additional difficulties.

State-Trait Emotions

Some emotions are reflected in the moment. They change depending on the situation. Others, however, may be old "companions" and more related to your unique personality. A *state emotion* is a feeling that is evoked in the present, while a *trait emotion* is a feeling that has been evoked many times in the past and is part of your history. This concept of *state-trait* emotions continues to be a major focus of research (Spielberger 1979). Of importance here is the relationship of your emotions, new or old, state or trait, to your world—and to your family relationships.

Family Affective Themes

Emotional legacies are emotionally charged themes that are transferred from generation to generation (Scarf 1995). Family transitions, such as marriage, the birth of children, retirement, and death, often stir hidden emotional legacies, or family affective themes. Just as you learn how to behave in certain situations from your family members, you also learn how to feel and react to information full of emotion.

One way that you, when you were a child, began to learn your place in the world was through your parents' eyes. You took to heart not only what they said but, more important, what they did. These messages affected your first feelings about yourself and became powerful forces in your life. These feelings grew within you as you reached adulthood and eventually were passed onto your own children.

Even your choice of life partner may be an unconscious attempt to re-create a family theme. Hendrix (1992) calls this theory the *imago* (Latin for "image"). This "shadow" of a past parent, which automatically appears when you choose your mate, may be the opposite sex parent and/or the parent with whom you have the most unresolved issues. In essence, your choice of a mate may be an attempt to get your unresolved childhood needs met. It may represent how your parents responded to your earliest needs. Just as in the old tale, *The Princess and the Pea*, wherein the princess was able to feel the pea through piles of mattresses, you may also be able to continue to feel the impact of your emotional baggage, no matter how much time passes, unless you do something about it.

Traumatic Experiences

Traumas can be large or small, brief or enduring, major or minor, intentional or accidental. If it was traumatic to you, it was a trauma. You, as an individual, determine what is or is not a trauma. What one person may perceive to be an unfortunate event may be devastating to someone else. If you experienced trauma at a certain stage in your life and did not adequately deal with your resulting feelings, it is likely that your children will experience similar traumas in their lives, and their children will experience the trauma, etc. Thus, a family pattern of not dealing with feelings evolves, even if there is no conscious intent.

Teasing is one example of a trauma. Chronic exposure to teasing can create situations where children, even adults, begin to display avoidant behaviors. You may not want to be around others, or you may begin to believe that others are talking about you, even when they are not. Another example of a trauma is accidentally tripping and falling in front of other people. This could make you overly self-conscious when you are in front of other people in the future and, in the extreme, could lead to social fear or anxiety. This creates a perception of the world that is not accurate or founded in "reality" and affects your ability to relate to others.

Traumas, however, are not the only experiences that affect your FATs. Even good or funny events contribute to your views of the world and your perceptions of yourself in it. Again, the event itself is not the most important factor in shaping your experience, but rather your perception of the event and your conclusion about it. Thus, perceptions can enhance traumatic FATs. This is why traumas must be resolved in order for you to fully develop into your RILEE potential and allow your children to grow as individuals. You must get rid of your FATs!

Get Rid of Your FATs!

How do you get rid of FATs? Once you begin to understand the part your FATs play in your children's development, you can make better choices. You will have the ability to recognize situations that could potentially create emotional baggage for your children. And you can stop it from happening! The goal is to change your *emotional baggage* to *feeling luggage*. One activity to help you achieve this is the RILEE Baggage Game, which you can play with your children. This game is not just for kids, even though it may seem that way. If you are eighteen or older, go back in time to somewhere between ages five and fifteen and join your children in the game.

RILEE Baggage Game

The following activity is meant to facilitate you and your children in sharing thoughts and feelings, so that you may better understand your family's emotional baggage. What exactly is the difference between baggage and luggage, anyway? Here, *baggage* is what is chosen for you, whereas *luggage* is something that you choose for yourself. The purpose of this exercise, therefore, is to help you learn how to choose what you want to carry around with you (or not!), rather than continue to lug around all those same old bags!

This RILEE Baggage Game will help you interact with one another. You play it by reading a scenario and discussing the thoughts, feelings, experiences, and memories the scenario evokes. In this way, you become aware of what you've been carrying and you help your children pack their luggage to meet the demands of their destination, which is better relating!

Directions: Read over the scenarios in the next few pages ahead of time. Please note that this game is organized according to age appropriateness level. Choose scenarios that seem most appropriate for your family.

Photocopy the pages with scenarios and cut along the dotted lines. Pick a card from the stack of cutouts and read the story out loud. Each family member should have an opportunity to answer the three questions that follow. Let yourself go last.

You will notice that the same three questions are asked for each scenario. These three questions are related to the cognitive behavioral "triangle" of thinking, feeling, and doing (Beck 1995). The main idea of this theory or model is that your perception of an event (e.g., thinking) affects your feeling, which in turn, affects what you do. By recognizing how you respond to certain situations, you will be better able to change your response.

For Younger Children (Ages Five to Eight)

Mary was called to the front of the class. On the way, she tripped on Johnny's book bag. She fell down in front of all of her classmates.

   a. What did she say to herself?

   b. How did she feel?

   c. What did she do afterwards?

Jack was late for his lesson, because his mother did not pick him up from school on time. When he arrived the instructor gave him extra work, because he was late.

   a. What did he say to himself?

   b. How did he feel?

   c. What did he do afterwards?

The game was tied with five seconds left and John missed the shot to win the game.

   a. What did he say to himself?

   b. How did he feel?

   c. What did he do afterwards?

Kisha lost her favorite doll. She looked everywhere for it, but could not find it.

   a. What did she say to herself?

   b. How did she feel?

   c. What did she do afterwards?

Larry thought he had made an A on his test. He had been bragging to Joe and saying, "I am so smart and you are not." When Larry got his test back he had made a much lower grade than Joe.

   a. What did he say to himself?

   b. How did he feel?

   c. What did he do afterwards?

Carolyn's parents told her that they would take her to her favorite theme park on Saturday. When Saturday came her parents had to go to a funeral. Carolyn did not get to go to the park.

   a. What did she say to herself?

   b. How did she feel?

   c. What did she do afterwards?

Jennifer wanted to play with her friends after school. Her parents told her that she could not play until she finished her homework. Jennifer began slamming doors in the house.

   a. What did she say to herself?

   b. How did she feel?

   c. What did she do afterwards?

Valencia found out that her dog Rocky was very sick. The veterinarian did not think Rocky would live very long.

   a. What did she say to herself?

   b. How did she feel?

   c. What did she do afterwards?

Maria, an immigrant child, was detained in her country for one week before coming to the United States. She is now in a public school for the very first time. She has just been sent to a behavior clinic for talking too much in class.

    a. What did she say to herself?

    b. How did she feel?

    c. What did she do afterwards?

Linda found her grandmother's favorite dress pin. Her grandmother told her she could keep it. Linda had always thought the pin was beautiful.

    a. What did she say to herself?

    b. How did she feel?

    c. What did she do afterwards?

Casey was asked to sing "The Star-Spangled Banner" in front of the whole school. She practiced for days. Casey overslept the day of the performance and missed it.

    a. What did she say to herself?

    b. How did she feel?

    c. What did she do afterwards?

Jane had the flu and went to the doctor. The doctor said she would need a shot and showed her the needle.

    a. What did she say to herself?

    b. How did she feel?

    c. What did she do afterwards?

Frank cleaned up his room without being told to do so. His parents rewarded him by taking him to the store and allowing him to choose his favorite toy.

    a. What did he say to himself?

    b. How did he feel?

    c. What did he do afterwards?

LaBrandon's parents gave him a Dalmatian puppy for his birthday. LaBrandon had been wanting one for a long, long time.

    a. What did he say to himself?

    b. How did he feel?

    c. What did he do afterwards?

For Older Children (Ages Nine to Twelve)

Billy watched a horror movie with his friends at the theater. That night he had a hard time falling asleep.

    a. What did he say to himself?

    b. How did he feel?

    c. What did he do afterwards?

Holly was on the way to visit her grandmother during her summer vacation. She had never been on a plane before. She held her teddy bear tightly during the entire flight.

    a. What did she say to herself?

    b. How did she feel?

    c. What did she do afterwards?

Cindy was on her way to a friend's house. While she was walking down the street, she heard a gunshot.

    a. What did she say to herself?

    b. How did she feel?

    c. What did she do afterwards?

Irene lent her favorite sweater to her friend. Her friend Janie spilled grape juice all over the sweater and returned it that way.

    a. What did she say to herself?

    b. How did she feel?

    c. What did she do afterwards?

Elizabeth went over to her friend's house for dinner. While she was there her friend's parents got into an argument and began speaking another language. They almost hit each other.

    a. What did she say to herself?

    b. How did she feel?

    c. What did she do afterwards?

Nathan had just moved to a new city. He was starting a new school, and he did not know any of the other children.

    a. What did he say to himself?

    b. How did he feel?

    c. What did he do afterwards?

Greg found out that he was having a pop quiz in his hardest subject today. He had not studied.

    a. What did he say to himself?

    b. How did he feel?

    c. What did he do afterwards?

Oscar's parents just informed him that they were getting a divorce.

    a. What did he say to himself?

    b. How did he feel?

    c. What did he do afterwards?

Patrick was at his friend's house. When they were playing, Patrick accidentally broke his friend's watch.

    a. What did he say to himself?

    b. How did he feel?

    c. What did he do afterwards?

Reginald and his parents were on the way to a soccer game when another car hit their car.

    a. What did he say to himself?

    b. How did he feel?

    c. What did he do afterwards?

Ms. Martin asked Robin a history question in class. Robin did not know the answer. Ms. Martin told her she needed to study more.

    a. What did she say to herself?

    b. How did she feel?

    c. What did she do afterwards?

Abby's best friend, Mary, was having a birthday party. All of Abby's friends would be there. Abby could not go because she had to baby-sit her one-year-old brother.

    a. What did she say to herself?

    b. How did she feel?

    c. What did she do afterwards?

Rebecca made the cheerleading squad. She had been practicing for months.

    a. What did she say to herself?

    b. How did she feel?

    c. What did she do afterwards?

Miguel was talking to his parents when they heard a loud noise. They looked outside and saw that a car had caught on fire.

    a. What did he say to himself?

    b. How did he feel?

    c. What did he do afterwards?

Jorge had the highest grades in the class. His teacher informed him that he would participate in the school rally because of his good grades.

    a. What did he say to himself?

    b. How did he feel?

    c. What did he do afterwards?

Marlon had climbed up on a tree branch. The branch was not strong enough, and it broke. He fell and hit the ground.

    a. What did he say to himself?

    b. How did he feel?

    c. What did he do afterwards?

RILEE Baggage Game Review

In the **RILEE Baggage Game**, you learned the types of things you say to yourself, how those things affect the way you feel, and the resulting behaviors. These insights will help you to better understand the emotional baggage that you have developed and inherited.

Checking Your Bags

Now that you have identified your emotional baggage, you can choose what you want to pack in your feeling *luggage*. Get ready to check your baggage—your emotional *baggage*! How do you do this?

One way that you can turn your baggage into luggage is by changing your behavior. Learning theory holds that your behaviors are reinforced or rewarded, and the outcome of your actions determines whether those actions will be repeated or not. This external motivation works and is often necessary. External motivation is defined as doing something that is based on an incentive that is outside of yourself.

Your goal, however, is to teach your children how to be *internally motivated*. This means that you want your children to do something that is based on an incentive that is deep inside of themselves, such as reading for pleasure. You want your children to develop an internal understanding so that they may take better care of themselves and not rely solely on externals. Think about it. Children already have lots of external controllers and motivators; peers, teacher, clergy, and yes, even you. External controls and motivations are necessary and even helpful. You want to supplement them, however, by helping your children to understand their choices and to make RILEE choices. This is when your children make decisions that benefit all people involved. What a positive difference this can make in their lives and your life!

You are essentially teaching *personal* responsibility and accountability. One way to develop these internal standards is to help your children learn to act in socially acceptable ways. By doing this, you get rid of some of the FATs. This next game will help you do just that.

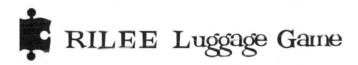

RILEE Luggage Game

To get rid of the FATs, you want to help your children make better choices for their *feeling* luggage. You want them to acquire wheels and straps to make their luggage easier to carry around. The RILEE Luggage Game will help develop healthier behaviors.

Directions: In this game you and your children will read aloud and respond to some of the same scenarios as those in the RILEE Baggage Game. Choose the scenarios that seem appropriate for you and your family. Try to discuss old and new solutions. Welcome input from all family members. Remember that it is okay to go back in time and play as if you were a child of five or an adolescent of fifteen. This will help your children realize that you also had to face these struggles.

Pick a comfortable area with good lighting. Read the stories on one of the next two pages. Choose one that you picked before. Remember your answers. Now, discuss what could have been done differently in each situation. The three questions that follow each story will help you restructure the thoughts that previously resulted in your baggage. This turns it into luggage, which is easier to manage.

For Younger Children (Ages Five to Eight)

Mary was called to the front of the class. On the way, she tripped on Johnny's book bag. She fell down in front of all of her classmates.

    a. How might she have thought differently?

    b. How might she have felt differently?

    c. How might she have behaved differently?

Carolyn's parents told her that they would take her to her favorite theme park on Saturday. When Saturday came, her parents had to go to a funeral. Carolyn did not get to go to the park.

    a. How might she have thought differently?

    b. How might she have felt differently?

    c. How might she have behaved differently?

Larry thought he had made an A on his test. He had been bragging to Joe and saying, "I am so smart, and you're not." When Larry got his test back, he had made a much lower grade than Joe.

    a. How might he have thought differently?

    b. How might he have felt differently?

    c. How might he have behaved differently?

Jennifer wanted to play with her friends after school. Her parents told her that she could not play until she finished her homework. Jennifer began slamming doors in the house.

    a. How might she have thought differently?

    b. How might she have felt differently?

    c. How might she have behaved differently?

For Older Children (Ages Nine to Twelve)

Billy watched a horror movie with his friends at the theater. That night he had a hard time falling asleep.

    a. How might he have thought differently?

    b. How might he have felt differently?

    c. How might he have behaved differently?

Abby's best friend, Mary, was having a birthday party. All of Abby's friends would be there. Abby could not go because she had to baby-sit her little brother.

    a. How might she have thought differently?

    b. How might she have felt differently?

    c. How might she have behaved differently?

Marlon had climbed up on a tree branch. The branch was not strong enough, and it broke. He fell and hit the ground.

    a. How might he have thought differently?

    b. How might he have felt differently?

    c. How might he have behaved differently?

Irene lent her favorite sweater to her friend. Her friend spilled grape juice all over the sweater and returned it that way.

    a. How might she have thought differently?

    b. How might she have felt differently?

    c. How might she have behaved differently?

RILEE Luggage Game Review

In this game you received some new tools to help you turn your emotional baggage into more manageable luggage. You recognized the way your thoughts affect your feelings and, ultimately, your behavior. This game took that concept one step further in asking you to change the way you think, which changes the way you feel and behave. These are your emotional straps and wheels!

These two games have started you and your children on a positive journey. When you learn how to make good choices in difficult situations, you are on your way to finding RILEE. When strong emotions are involved, however, it is easy to take the angry path. Remember these exercises and get on the RILEE path. This path will allow you to deal with your strong new feelings in spite of those old emotional memories.

Remember to use emotional helpers and to avoid emotional stoppers.

Helpers (What to Practice)	Stoppers (What to Avoid)
1. Permission to share feelings	1. Ridicule
2. Positive gestures	2. Punishment
3. Family discussion	3. Harsh words
4. Citing behaviors rather than making judgments	4. Ignoring a child's needs
5. Hugs/kisses	5. Verbal and nonverbal cutoffs (saying "Shut up," rolling your eyes)
6. Giving praise	6. Silence
7. Speaking softly	7. Yelling

Reminder: Old emotional memories can have a powerful effect on your ability to make changes. In fact, often what prevents you from choosing a RILEE outcome is one or more of your family affective themes.

chapter 3

The Six Types
of FAT

FAT! What is it? Fat is a compound occurring in a person's connective tissue. It grows and grows, adding weight and inches. By FAT, we mean a heavy psychological compound, or feeling, that interferes with a person's ability to relate. FAT certainly gets in the way.

It takes a long, long time for FATs to build up in your family's emotional system. It comes from years, perhaps even generations, of relating the wrong way. Eventually, it weighs your family down—way down. Then talking, sharing, and caring become very, very hard, especially in difficult times. It is important to stop the passage of FATs from one generation to another.

The Importance of a Healthy Diet

You are reading this workbook because your family is important to you. Every family member is precious. Giving them the right psychological nutrition is just as important as giving them the right physical nutrition. You would never serve your family a diet high in fat. Yet you might unknowingly be offering your family a psychological diet high in FATs!

It is hard enough to deal with the present-state emotions that you feel. But when you add past-trait emotions comprised of stored-up FATs to the mixture, the experience becomes overwhelming. You might believe that you have all of your past-trait emotions under tight lock and key, that you are in control. But, in a moment of crisis, there they come flooding in.

The Importance of a Good Offense

The best defense against a FATs flood is a good offense. Understanding your emotional history will help you to be prepared, to initiate action rather than to react to it. That is the difference between offense and defense.

Remember the old saying: Knowledge is power. This is true. This chapter is all about knowing. When you know what has been and what is, you can initiate a powerful offensive action, even under pressure.

First, you must understand some basic developmental concepts that can offer a meaningful perspective. Having a good frame of reference is crucial to flexibility. Without this knowledge, you may repeat your family's affective history. Keep in mind that the goal is to eliminate the FATs.

Understanding Trait Images

The first requirement to eliminate the FATs is to understand the trait images that are interfering with your choices. Sometimes you may do things and not even know why you made the choice you made. Yet, you know that the choice you made was familiar—very, very familiar. It is important to recognize that, just because a choice or feeling is familiar, doesn't mean that it is a good choice.

This chapter will address the six most common family affective themes—fear, anger, anxiety, embarrassment, sadness, and happiness—and how they originate.

Understanding Developmental Stages

There are many stages of development that each child must successfully complete in order to stay on the RILEE path. Parental validation is a must, as children learn by imitation, experience, and example along the way. Such helper phrases as, "You are doing a great job," and "I like the way you handled that," are examples of validation. Children need for you as a parent to mirror, guide, and direct their progress so that they don't get wounded or stuck along the way. Many theorists have studied child development. We have chosen to highlight *imago theory* (Hendrix 1988, 1992).

Hendrix's First Imago Stage

The goal of the first imago stage (which happens in the first eighteen months of life) is *attachment* (Hendrix 1992, 63–74). If you properly bonded with your mother and do not experience trauma during this period, you can move on without unfinished business. If, however, there are problems, this is when we believe the *scary* FATs begin. These problems show up in either clinging or avoiding behaviors. As adults, *clingers* and *avoiders* often pair up as couples. And, according to our RILEE theory, they produce *scared* children.

Are your children easily frightened? Are they afraid to attach? Are they afraid you won't be there for them? Are they afraid you will leave them behind? Are you afraid? Are they afraid? Then *fear* is your FATs theme.

Scared families are afraid to do practically everything. They don't want to take any risks. They do not understand comfort. Life revolves around becoming secure, a process which is never fully achieved.

Hendrix's Second Imago Stage

The goal of the second imago stage (eighteen months to three years) is *exploration* (Hendrix 1992, 75–83). In this stage, you explore your world and reattach to your mother over and over again. If you do so and do not experience trauma during this period, you can move on without unfinished business. If, however, there are problems, this is when we believe the *angry* FATs begin. These problems show up in either pursuing or isolating behaviors. As adults, *pursuers* and *isolators* often pair up. And, according to our RILEE theory, they produce *angry* children.

Are your children easily angered? Are they afraid of loss? Are they afraid of being smothered? Are they afraid to anger you? Are you afraid to anger them? Then anger is your FATs theme!

The *angry* family is a family that has trouble with friendship. This family would rather have battles than give hugs. Instead of a healthy expression of feelings (i.e., attention, acceptance, approval, acknowledgement, and affection), there is a hostile expression of feelings. Thus, disapproving, rejecting, ignoring, and frustrated behaviors are par for the course.

Hendrix's Third Imago Stage

The goal of the third imago stage (three to four years of age) is *identity* (Hendrix 1992, 84–93). During this stage you need to separate from your parents and define yourself as unique and different from them. If you do so and do not experience trauma during this period, you can move on without unfinished business. If, however, there are problems during this period, this is when we believe the *anxious* FATs begin. These problems show up in either controlling or diffusing behaviors. As adults, *controllers* and *diffusers* often pair up. And, according to our RILEE theory, they produce *anxious* children.

Are your children anxious? Are they afraid of being shamed? Are they afraid to become their own person? Do they continue to live in your shadow? Do they have physical signs of anxiety (e.g., shaking, sweating, stuttering)? Do they have performance anxiety? Do they work hard without results? Do you work hard without results? Then *anxiety* is your FATs theme!

The *anxious* family is a family that is always waiting for the other shoe to drop, afraid to be calm, to relax and enjoy life. In a scared family, security and survival come first, but in an anxious family, safety and responsibility come first. Fun is not okay.

Hendrix's Fourth Imago Stage

The goal of the fourth imago stage (four to seven years of age) is *competence* (Hendrix 1992, 94–99). In this stage you need to learn how to compete and win, to be seen as competent rather than defective. If you do so and do not experience trauma during this period, you can move on without unfinished business. If, however, there are problems during this period, this is when we believe the *embarrassed* FATs begin. As adults, *competitors* and *manipulators* often pair up. And, according to our RILEE theory, they produce *embarrassed* children.

Are your children easily embarrassed? Are they afraid to be in the spotlight? Are they required to keep secrets? Do you keep secrets? Then *embarrassment* is your FATs theme!

The *embarrassed* family avoids attention. Both accomplishments and failures are avoided. This is a family of secrets. Instead of family members connecting to the world, they become enmeshed with one another.

Hendrix's Fifth Imago Stage

The goal of the fifth Imago Stage (seven to thirteen years of age) is *concern* (Hendrix 1992, 100–106). This is when you need to learn how to belong to a group outside of your family structure. If you do so and do not experience trauma during this period, you can move on without unfinished business. If, however, there are problems during this period, this is when we believe the *sad* FATs begin. As adults, people with sad FATs become *caretakers* and *loners* and they often pair up. According to our RILEE theory, they produce *sad* children.

Are your children sad? Are they afraid of the dark? Are they afraid to play by themselves? Do they want to take care of you? Are they overattached to computers and electronics and underattached to people and pets? Do they spend all their spare time under headphones listening to strange music? Then *sadness* is your FATs theme.

The *sad* family can sometimes have a genetic predisposition toward depression that's not understood. Sometimes there can be an overwhelming sense of gloom. Some families are sad because of circumstances or tragedies that they don't know how to handle. Often, feeling anything other than sadness may seem wrong.

Hendrix's Sixth Imago Stage

The goal of the sixth Imago Stage (thirteen to nineteen) is *intimacy* (Hendrix 1992, 106–114). Here you need to learn to be different from your family and/or your peers. If you achieve this goal and do not experience trauma during this period, you can move on without unfinished business. If, however, there are problems, this is when we believe the *happy* FATs begin. As adults, people with happy FATs become *rebels* and *conformists*, and they often pair up. According to our RILEE theory, they produce children who are *very happy—too happy*.

Are your children *too* happy? Are they afraid to express any feelings other than happiness? Do you discourage other feelings? Do you insist on having one big happy family? Do you have any introverts in your family? (An introvert is a person who needs to spend considerable time alone and/or with things; whereas an extrovert is a person who needs to spend considerable time with others and/or pets.) Do the extroverts in your family show tolerance for the introverts and vice versa? Are your family members prone to smile too much because they are trying to hide their feelings? Then *happiness* is your FATs theme.

The *happy* family can be both a joy and a curse. If a family is too happy, then there can be too much togetherness, especially for an introverted child.

The Seventh Stage—The Age of RILEE Choices

The goal of, perhaps, a seventh stage of development, the RILEE Stage, is *choice*. When you create joy, maintain a balanced emotional state, and generate productive thoughts and behaviors consistently over time, then you have chosen the RILEE path.

Your Freedom to Choose

You can choose to resolve emotional traumas. FATs restrict growth. They thwart the developmental process. You have a right to keep your FATs, but exercising more connective behaviors frees you to develop. The goal is to exercise attachment security, attention, acceptance, approval, acknowledgement, and affection, by maintaining a healthy diet of balanced emotions.

Give Attachment Security

To resolve stage one attachment traumas, you must create *comfort* in your family. Comfort involves inviting all to feel safe and secure. Comfort requires good visual, auditory, and touching cues and very positive thoughts and communications. Your children must feel wanted. When children feel safe and wanted, then they can bond. Even in stage one, children know if you want them and if you are truly committed to their well-being. When they do not sense this offer of attachment, they will not bond to you. Resolving any ambivalence you might have toward your children, your mate, and your family is the greatest gift of *attachment security* you can offer.

You may find the following list of *comfort* helpers and *scary* stoppers useful. Please add three helpers and stoppers that are unique to your family.

Comfort Helpers

1. Looking at your child and smiling

2. Making loving, affirming statements

3. Singing lullabies

4. Touching your child often

5. Cuddling your child

6. Holding your child close to your heart

7. Perceiving your child as a treasure

8. _____

9. _____

10. _____

Scary Stoppers

1. Avoiding eye contact

2. Speaking harshly

3. Singing loudly

4. Leaving your child alone for extended periods

5. Letting your child scream for a long time

6. Allowing yourself to have mixed feelings toward your child

7. Perceiving your child as a burden

8. _____

9. _____

10. _____

Give Positive Attention

To resolve stage two exploration issues, you must create a *friendly* family environment. Teaching your children how to be real friends is a necessary part of the socialization process. A. F. Newcomb and C. L. Bagwell remind us that friendships are characterized by the following:

✳ "reciprocity and intimacy"

＊ "more intense social activity"

＊ "more frequent conflict resolution"

＊ "more effective task performance" (Smith, Cowie, and Blades 1998, 121).

Even though these behaviors mature and blend by stage seven, the groundwork for these characteristics is laid here in stage two. How are you demonstrating these four characteristics? Remember, your children are learning through imitation during this stage. Forget the concept of the terrible twos; ignore the tantrums. Concentrate on role modeling true friendship. Start with your mate. There is no substitute for polite and courteous behavior over time. During stage two, giving this gift of *positive attention* is your job!

You may find the following list of *friendly* helpers and *angry* stoppers useful. Please add three helpers and stoppers that are unique to your family.

Friendly Helpers	**Angry Stoppers**
1. Speaking softly	1. Yelling
2. Rewarding what is right	2. Punishing what is wrong
3. Treating all family members politely	3. Treating all family members rudely
4. Role modeling good behavior	4. Role modeling bad behavior
5. Watching your child imitate your good behavior	5. Watching your child imitate your bad behavior
6. Smiling when your child imitates your good behavior	6. Smiling when your child imitates your bad behavior
7. Telling your child how wonderful s/he is	7. Telling your child how terrible s/he is
8. _____	8. _____
9. _____	9. _____
10. _____	10. _____

Give Acceptance

To resolve stage three identity issues, you need to create a *calming* atmosphere. Learning how to keep yourself calm and rewarding your children for keeping themselves calm is your job. Develop a family phrase that invites/reminds all to keep calm (e.g., CALM: Comfort And Love Mix). Remember that anxiety is the opposite of calmness. Anxiety is not good for you or your family. It is also not necessary. Anxiety is usually created when you tell your children that they don't measure up, that they are not good enough, that they are stupid, that they are not your hoped-for children. Remember, you must be very careful with your words and your gestures. Children know when they do not measure up in your eyes. They then come to believe that they are defective and that they will never measure up in anyone else's eyes. Allow yourself to be pleased with who they are and who they are becoming. Give your children the gift of *acceptance*. In stage three, this is your job!

You may find the following list of *calm* helpers and *anxious* stoppers useful. Please add three helpers and stoppers that are unique to your family.

Calm Helpers	Anxious Stoppers
1. Sending positive messages: "You are so wonderful."	1. Sending negative messages: "You don't measure up"
2. Making positive gestures	2. Making negative gestures
3. Giving kisses	3. Frowning
4. Smiling with your eyes	4. Rolling your eyes
5. Being pleased with your child's behavior	5. Being disgusted with your child's behavior
6. Seeing your child as good	6. Seeing your child as bad
7. Remembering what your child does right	7. Remembering what your child does wrong
8. _____	8. _____
9. _____	9. _____
10. _____	10. _____

Give Approval

To resolve stage four competence issues, creating an atmosphere of *pride* is the goal. Help your children feel proud of themselves. Teach your children to feel comfortable in the spotlight. Allow your children to perform adequately, not perfectly, for the family and for others. These are all important rites of passage. Your children need to feel competent. Your children need to feel special. Your children need to be praised for their successes, but not to be reprimanded for their failures. Your children must learn that experiencing failure is an essential part of becoming competent. Children who are never allowed to fail become very fragile adults. Likewise, children who are never allowed to succeed never become adults at all. In stage four, giving the gift of *approval* is your job!

You may find the following list of *proud* helpers and *embarrassed* stoppers useful. Please add three helpers and stoppers that are unique to your family.

Proud Helpers	Embarrassed Stoppers
1. Sending approving messages: "You did that well."	1. Sending disapproving messages: "You messed up."
2. Praising your child with your gestures	2. Punishing your child with your gestures
3. Encouraging your child to be open	3. Encouraging your child to keep secrets
4. Encouraging your child to participate	4. Discouraging your child from participating
5. Allowing your child to fail	5. Allowing only success

Proud Helpers	Embarrassed Stoppers
6. Refraining from evaluating your child's efforts	6. Judging all of your child's efforts
7. Seeing your child as competent	7. Seeing your child as incompetent
8. _____	8. _____
9. _____	9. _____
10. _____	10. _____

Give Acknowledgment

To resolve stage five concern issues, creating an atmosphere of *gladness* is the goal. Allowing your children to feel glad when they strive to belong is very important. If they want to learn to play the drums in order to be in the band, if they want to take karate because their best friends are doing so, if they want to wear their hair a different way, so what! Does everything really have to be your way? If it does, you are thwarting their development. When this happens, your children will become very sad. How can they belong without acknowledgment? You must acknowledge their desire for belonging, even though it is perhaps displayed in a way that is different from your values and beliefs. Remember, you can acknowledge your children's choices without approving of them. Withholding acknowledgement can produce enormous sadness and disappointment within the family. In stage five, giving the gift of *acknowledgment* is your job!

You may find the following list of *glad* helpers and *sad* stoppers useful. Please add three helpers and stoppers that are unique to your family.

Glad Helpers	Sad Stoppers
1. Allowing your child to belong to groups outside of the family	1. Preventing your child from belonging to groups outside of the family
2. Allowing your child to learn new things	2. Preventing your child from learning new things
3. Sharing control	3. Remaining in control
4. Allowing your child to be different from you	4. Demanding that your child follow in your footsteps
5. Being satisfied with your child	5. Being disappointed in your child
6. Understanding that acknowledgment and approval are different	6. Seeing acknowledgement and approval as the same
7. Expecting your child to investigate different values and beliefs	7. Demanding that your child maintain the family's values and beliefs without question
8. _____	8. _____
9. _____	9. _____
10. _____	10. _____

Give Affection

To resolve stage six intimacy issues, freeing your family from the "happy" fix and allowing *gloomy* feelings to be present as well is very important. If your children have to be happy all the time, how can they be real? Being *real* is feeling all feelings, but in balance. *Remember, love is not about being happy; it is about being real.* And that is where RILEE theory comes in. Sometimes the appearance of love can be truly gloomy. For example, your children need to be free to feel gloomy when a member of your family is very sick and about to die. Sometimes that gloomy form of love is the tie that binds. It allows you and your children to be real. In stage six, giving the gift of real *affection* is your job!

You may find the following list of *gloomy* helpers and *happy* stoppers useful. Please add three helpers and stoppers that are unique to your family.

Gloomy Helpers

1. Allowing your child to be real

2. Telling your child that being loving is about feeling many feelings

3. Creating balance

4. Giving your child the freedom of expression

5. Allowing family members to attach and detach as needed

6. Allowing family members to be different

7. Encouraging independence

8. _____

9. _____

10. _____

Happy Stoppers

1. Demanding that your child maintain a façade

2. Telling your child that being loving is about feeling only one feeling—happy

3. Forcing smiles

4. Denying your child the freedom of expression

5. Keeping all family members tightly connected

6. Demanding the same behaviors of all family members

7. Encouraging dependence

8. _____

9. _____

10. _____

The Six Gifts of Love

Remember, these are the gifts you must give your children. They are the gifts of

1. attachment security

2. attention

3. acceptance

4. approval

5. acknowledgement

6. affection

These are the six RILEE A's. They are free. When you give freely, you will receive freely. And the gifts you receive will be the most precious gifts of all—because they will come from your children.

Be Prepared to Repeat the Process

With the addition of our RILEE theory, you now know how to help yourself and your children master each of Hendrix's imago developmental stages. But according to Luquet (1996), the process of moving through these stages occurs over and over again during your life. Be prepared to repeat the process!

Paul Baltes and his colleagues suggested that there are three influences on beginning and repeating a developmental cycle (Smith, Cowie, Blades 1998). The first is a *biological* influence, which is basically age dependent. For example, when you are born, you automatically enter developmental stage one. The second is the *historical* influence, which is basically tied to important discoveries and advances. For example, when the computer became a significant part of family life, everyone reentered developmental stage one—shall I become attached to this new invention or not? The third is the *environmental* influence, which is basically tied to unexpected or traumatic life events.

Learn through Play

And then there's play! Are you remembering the importance of play? When your children enter Hendrix's developmental stage two, *exploration*, according to C. Hutt, they begin to explore, finding out "what does this object do?" and play, finding out "what can I do with this object?" (Smith, Cowie, and Blades 1998, 201). Do you remember how to play? Being a RILEE adult does not mean giving up play. It means giving up ambivalence. Your work experiences need to be balanced with your family experiences, which need to be balanced with your play experiences. Think of a triangle with equal sides in which these different parts of your life find balance.

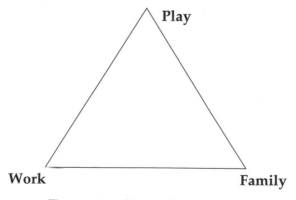

Figure 3.1 Work, Play, and Family

Play allows growth and relieves pressure. Playing the RILEE way involves variety, enjoyment, fantasy, and internal cues. Playing the angry way, however, involves monotony, seriousness, reality, and external cues. In the RILEE setting, families are having fun when they play together. It is important to understand the difference between play and homework, jamming and practicing, storytelling and reading assignments, and doing things for fun versus doing things for a reward.

So, remember that playing with your children is investing in them. Playing calms their anxieties and allows them to develop mastery. According to Susan Isaacs, play is "essential to both emotional and cognitive growth of young children" (Smith, Cowie, and Blades 1998, 194). Play is about relaxing, diversifying, creating, and fantasizing. Play is indeed an encouraging RILEE process!

Now that you have become acquainted with Hendrix's imago developmental theory, now that you know how to create a balanced emotional state via our RILEE theory, and now that you understand the importance of play as a medium for growth and change, you are ready to move to chapter 4. Please have your family join you in learning to create a healthy RILEE family. Remember, creating joy is a very ordinary process; it is within your grasp. We ask that you invite all members of your family to join in this playful RILEE experience.

chapter 4

Creating a Healthy RILEE Family

In chapter 3, you learned about the different types of family affective themes (FATs) that can affect your family's relating experiences. As you already know, having too much of one feeling is unhealthy. There must be a balance. This chapter will help you reduce your FAT and help your family create a balance through exploration and play.

The healthy family has all of the six types of FAT or feelings in perspective—no one family affective theme dominates. Therefore, within this family, all feelings are allowed, as long as they are expressed properly. Anger is the most problematic feeling to express properly. Some families hold anger in and never resolve it. Other families let their anger out and create more problems. Healthy emotional expression resolves problems. Review your family affective themes in the following activity! You and your family may either copy this exercise or use a blank sheet of paper to record your responses.

The Family Affective Theme Worksheet

Get comfortable and relax. In the spaces provided below, respond to the following:

1. Think back to your first memory involving family members (this can be any memory at all involving any of your five senses). What do you remember?

_____

_____

2. Describe your feelings during this memory (what you remember feeling at the time of the experience).

_____

_____

3. Now remember other times when you felt the following six FAT feelings:

scared _____

_____

angry _____

_____

anxious _____

_____

embarrassed _____

_____

sad _____

_____

happy _____

_____

Expressing Emotions

Healthy emotional expression involves sharing your feelings without deliberately hurting yourself or someone else. How do you express emotions in your family? Do you create joy or do you create pain?

In a healthy RILEE family, sharing real feelings in a respectful way can lead to resolution. Resolution creates joy, even if that resolution is difficult. Having things resolved provides amazing relief and offers an opportunity to become closer. Remember a time when you kept a secret that was building up inside of you. Finally, you felt safe enough to share it. Even though it was difficult to do, you experienced joy when the task was accomplished. For example, did you ever break one of your mother's prized vases and then feel guilty about it, especially because you knew that nobody saw you do it? How did you handle the sadness in your mother's eyes when she saw the pieces on the floor? Was it better when you talked it out? Or, did you create pain by withholding this information and allowing your mother to feel sad? Perhaps another family member was blamed. How did you feel—getting away with something at the expense of others?

What is the family affective theme in the example given above? Were you scared? Was your mom sad? Was anyone angry? Or did one feeling dominate? Was that feeling a general tone of sadness? If so, then your family affective theme was *sadness*. Did you resolve this theme or is it still with you? Remember that resolution involves *acknowledgment*. In this example, acknowledgment means taking responsibility for your own behavior. When you take responsibility and acknowledge your role in the family, you begin to deal with the emotions that are prevalent in your family.

As you reviewed the broken vase example, did you remember something similar? Was it dealt with in a respectful way, or were there leftover emotional wounds? By acknowledging that you did something and accepting the consequences for it, you are opening up emotional communication within your family and dealing with your family affective themes.

You have probably experienced all six family affective themes at some time or other while growing up. Some families, however, rely on only one or two main emotions to deal with their problems. Therefore, these families have an unhealthy affective history that prevents resolution. They may be just creating more problems for themselves. A healthy family allows all emotions on the RILEE continuum to be expressed within the household in a respectful way.

Our next focus will be on overcoming your dominant family affective themes and creating and maintaining a healthy balance—allowing yourself and your children to experience all emotions on the continuum. Remember that RILEE theory involves:

1. creating comfort in the family,

2. creating a friendly environment,

3. creating a calming atmosphere,

4. creating an atmosphere of pride,

5. creating an atmosphere of gladness, and

6. allowing gloomy feelings within the family.

Creating joy every day in your family is the heart of a healthy RILEE family. The next activity will give you more practice.

Sharing Your Feelings

Review your answers on the family affective theme worksheet. Pick two or three of your strongest memories, those that impressed you most. Now take turns sharing them with your family members. You may wish to list memories that were strong for different family members in the space provided.

_____

_____

_____

_____

_____

_____

_____

_____

_____

_____

_____

_____

_____

_____

_____

_____

_____

_____

_____

Promoting Empathy

The next activity illustrates how each family member may perceive the same experience in different ways. Experiencing different feelings from those of others in the same family is a healthy process and should be encouraged, as long as the expression of these feelings is respectful of all family members. So, be open-minded! This process of recognizing and understanding others' viewpoints is important in promoting empathy. Empathy is simply putting yourself in someone else's shoes. Building empathy in your family is another way of creating a healthy RILEE family.

Understanding Different Views Worksheet

Have each family member pick from the previous worksheets one or two memories that include all members in the family. This may include a family vacation, baseball game, or major argument or conflict in the family. For each memory that is chosen, ask each family member to explain the feeling(s) he or she associates with that memory. List these responses in the spaces below. You may want to copy this page so each family member can participate.

Memory

Feeling

_____   _____

_____   _____

_____   _____

_____   _____

_____   _____

_____   _____

_____   _____

_____   _____

_____   _____

_____   _____

You may have noticed that in a given situation, one family member felt scared, while another felt angry. This is okay! The key is the healthy expression of the emotion, not the emotion itself. In discussing your feelings with family members, create a calm atmosphere. As you model empathy for your children, you will encourage them to develop empathy for others.

Now that you have practiced creating a healthy family through the activities in this chapter, you are on your way to relating in love every evening.

RILEE Bear in the Box Game

The purpose of the RILEE Bear in the Box Game is to help you create a healthy RILEE family by restructuring your FATs. Instead of operating on one extreme or the other of an emotional continuum, you need to learn to operate in the middle. In this game, the goal is to help the RILEE bear get out of the box.

Directions: Pick a comfortable area with good lighting. First, have every member in your family pick a number from one to five. Whatever you choose will be that of the stone on which you will land on the path to the box. You will use this same number for the first ten stones that are numbered.

Next, color in the first five stones with a crayon or magic marker: Color the first stone black, the second stone green, the third stone red, the fourth stone yellow, and the fifth stone red again. Then color the second set of five stones: Color the first stone green, the second stone black, the third stone yellow, the fourth stone red, and the fifth stone black again. Color the third set of five stones red. Color the fourth set of five stones yellow. Finally, color the fifth set of five stones green. The colors represent the different categories of feelings that can either stop a family from progressing (i.e., *red* is for *stopper*), keep the family in neutral (i.e., *yellow* is for *neutral*), or help the family move forward (i.e., *green* for *helper*). The black color is used as a wild card (which can be used as whatever color the player wishes) in this game.

The first ten stones: Have one member read the accompanying scenarios out loud. Invite members to answer and discuss the two scenarios according to the color of the stone on which they landed. Remember—red generates a *stopper* response, yellow a *neutral* response, and green a *helper* response.

The next color stones (red, yellow, green): For each of the next three scenarios, invite family members to respond, again based on the color of the stones. By the time you've discussed the last scenario, you will understand that the way you respond leads to different results. Since you've moved forward with *helper* responses, you win the game! RILEE bear is out of the box!

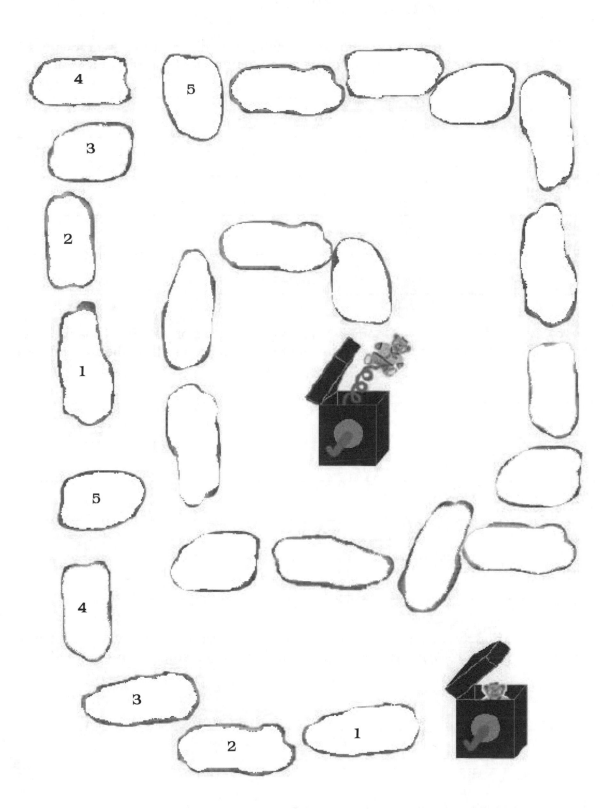

Scenarios

The first five stones. You and your family are planning a family vacation. Everyone has a different idea in mind. Invite family members to list and discuss their vacation choices.

_____

_____

_____

_____

_____

The next five stones. You and your family have only one television set. Everyone wants to watch a different show. Invite family members to list and discuss how they would deal with this.

_____

_____

_____

_____

_____

The red stones. Your child came home with a D on his/her report card. Invite each family member to generate a *stopper* response. (For example, "How stupid can you be?")

_____

_____

_____

_____

_____

The yellow stones. You and your family have just finished eating dinner. Everyone knows to help clean up; however, after dinner everyone goes their separate ways, leaving you with all the work. Invite each family member to generate a *neutral* response, rather than try to resolve the problem. (For example, "I'll do it later.")

_____

_____

_____

_____

_____

The green stones. Your family pet is sick. Invite each family member to generate a *helper* response. (For example, "I will go to the vet with you.")

_____

_____

_____

_____

_____

Now that you have met RILEE Bear, you will have some help in moving through the rest of this workbook. RILEE Bear teaches families to *relate in love every evening*. He is a most encouraging bear!

PART II

Good Teaching: The First Four Steps

Are you prepared to be a good teacher? Did you know that being a good parent involves being a good teacher? Do you know how to guide your children in their emotional and intellectual development? Are you really prepared to help them to learn to understand the myriad of confusing thoughts, feelings, and sensations within them? Do you understand how to guide them to wise actions? Can you help them deal with their anger?

In Part II, you will obtain a perspective that will make understanding thoughts, feelings, sensations, and actions much easier. You will learn how anger works. You will learn to recognize your anger. You will learn to control your anger. You will also learn the special skills that will prepare you to teach your children effective anger management.

chapter 5

Understanding the FACTS

Did you know that four important factors contribute to the choices you make? They are *feeling*, *acting*, *thinking*, and *sensing*. These factors help you in *choosing* wisely. When only one or two of these factors is involved in a decision, unwise choices are often made. But feeling, acting, choosing, thinking, and sensing together gives you the FACTS.

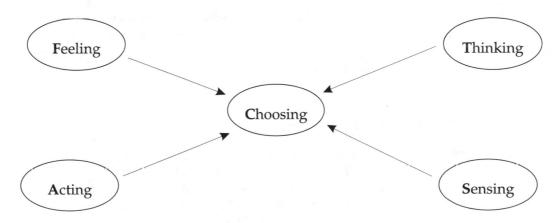

Figure 5.1 The FACTS

The Choices You Make

You may have heard of the expression, "Oops! Monday morning quarterbacking." This is when people review the plays from the previous weekend's game on Monday. Well, it doesn't just have to be about football. Revisiting old choices can be a good way for parents to use what they learn to make better choices in the future.

Do a "Monday morning quarterbacking" and revisit a time when you just reacted without thinking. Allow yourself to go back in time: 1) See the moment. 2) Remember who was there. 3) Remember what you did. Write it down. For example,

1. Charlie, my son, brought home his report card with a C in math.

2. Charlie, my husband, Dan, and I were there.

3. I yelled at Charlie for making a C in math.

Now come up with an example from your own experience.

1. _____

_____

2. _____

_____

3. _____

_____

Perhaps you might have remembered that your stomach was doing flips or your lower back was tightening up or your jaw was clenching. Most likely, your *body* was *sensing* a problem. Perhaps you were *feeling* something. Most likely you were revisiting some old emotional baggage. Perhaps your immediate state reaction was just like an old trait reaction from years ago.

By *acting* without *thinking*, for that is what a reaction is, you just create more problems for yourself and your family. This reactive form of parenting is a disaster. It assumes that no growth or change is occurring in your family. Yet your family and your children are constantly growing and changing.

Same Behavior, Different Meaning

It is important to know that a past behavior, although similar to a present behavior, may have a vastly different meaning. For example, when a two-year-old asks "Why?" it may be for very different reasons than when a seven-year-old asks "Why?"

In his imago developmental theory, Hendrix (1992) identifies a two-year-old as an explorer; whereas, a seven-year-old is busy striving for competence.

The Explorer

Two-year-olds often ask "Why?" as a way of feeling separate from their parents. As a parent, you want your child to learn and grow, and you encourage your child to explore his/her surroundings. When your child does this, however, you may find the constant barrage of questions annoying. You may *react* with anger. Your two-year-old is most likely just trying to get your friendly attention to show you his separateness. Yet he or she got you angry instead! Your child, who tried, was just tied. You created a double bind for your child. See figure 5.2.

> Explore.
>
> Don't explore.

Figure 5.2 Double Bind Box

Usually, such restrictive reactions are about you, the parent, not about your child. Your child, however, is the one who gets wounded. To prevent such double binds from occurring, the following helper responses are offered. You may wish to write in a few of your own as well.

1. "I love when you ask why."

2. "It is okay to explore."

3. "Yes, you are different from me and that is okay."

4. "After I finish this activity, I will come and listen to you."

5. _____

6. _____

7. _____

Please avoid the following *stopper* reactions. They are very wounding. So that you can make better choices, write in a few of your own as well.

1. "Stop asking me why!"

2. "Stop following me around!"

3. "You're driving me crazy."

4. "Don't do that."

5. _____

6. _____

7. _____

Masters in the Making

Seven-year-olds are frequently excited about learning to do something. They are often seeking your guidance and approval. You must be a good teacher. By reacting negatively (acting without thinking), you embarrass your child. You may also have sent the message, "You can't do it," when your child simply made a mistake. Children must be allowed to try and fail, in order to achieve mastery (competence). If they get punished for their efforts, they will sense your disapproval. You will have created another double bind box (see figure 5.3), and your children will have learned that they don't measure up.

You can do it.

You can't do it.

Figure 5.3 Double Bind Box

To prevent such double binds and their wounds, the following *helper* responses are offered. You may wish to write in a few of your own responses as well.

1. "I like the way you are doing that."

2. "Mistakes are okay. I make them, too."

3. "You are on the right path."

4. "Keep working at it. You've almost got it."

5. _____

6. _____

7. _____

Remember, be a good teacher. Respond, rather than react. Avoid these *stopper* reactions. They are very wounding. So that you can make better choices, write in a few of your own as well.

1. "You are so stupid."

2. "How could you embarrass me like that?"

3. "When are you going to get it right?"

4. "This is awful."

5. _____

6. _____

7. _____

Reactions vs. Responses

It is important for you and your family to replace hurtful reactions with healthy responses. *Reacting* is acting based on sensing or feeling, but without thinking. Reacting is usually based on incomplete facts. *Responding* is choosing an action based on sensing, feeling, and thinking. It is a matter of considering the complete facts. Taking the time to understand the feelings, actions, thoughts, and senses that go with a healthy choice avoids a lot of Monday morning quarterbacking.

Now that you understand the importance of the FACTS, it's time to teach them to your children.

Family Time

Remember RILEE? He's the bear that you got out of the box in chapter 4. Have you ever met a bear named RILEE before? Probably not. RILEE is a most unusual bear. His name stands for **r**elating **i**n **l**ove **e**very **e**vening. We call him RILEE for short. He is a re-lax-a-tion bear, and he is here to help you become RILEE, too.

RILEE Bear has come to join you and your family to play the RILEE Bear FACTS Game. This game will help all of you to *respond* rather than *react*. Understanding the FACTS will promote a lot of RILEE experiences. More mastery, less pain for everyone.

Before you play the Bear Facts Game, it will help to do the next exercise with the family.

Exercise 5.1

RILEE Bear Considers the FACTS

"Hi, I'm the facts-finding RILEE bear. I'm here to teach you that healthy responding is all about finding the FACTS. When I was just a bear in a box, I didn't understand this. I was always boxed in by a double bind message that said 'Stop. No, go' or a message that said 'Go. But be cautious.'" This is what RILEE Bear's box looks like:

> Stop.
> No, go.

or

> Go.
> But be cautious.

"There were so many *red* and *yellow* paths that I hardly ever could find the *green* path. Thank goodness for you and your family. You got me out of the box!

"Now, I'm here to help you find the FACTS. I can tell you that, before you came along, I spent many years in that box reacting, not responding. But now I know the difference. And I want to help you learn how to choose healthy responses too."

In this exercise everyone in the family should write down an example of a situation or an experience where it was hard to choose what to do. But before you think about this, here's an example of a situation in which the RILEE bear had a hard time choosing what to do.

RILEE Bear's Choices

The RILEE bear was accepted to three summer camps. The bear said: "My parents say this is my choice. Which one should I choose?"

1. "One is a soccer camp. I can learn how to play soccer better and spend a lot of time with other kids who are first string soccer team players at my school. Soccer is my most favorite sport, and I would love to be a first string player. My dad would like this."

2. "Another is a new music camp where I can learn to play the drums and practice being in the school marching band. I have a lot of friends at school who play in the band. My mom would like this."

3. "Or I can go to the same neighborhood camp that I went to last year. I can play a little soccer, but probably not much because everybody sees me as a real bench warmer. Yes, I must admit that I do a very good job of bench-warming. A lot of my friends will be there. I had a lot of fun there last year."

"So how do I make a healthy choice? By finding the FACTS."

"Choosing really is not easy. Should I please mom, dad, or myself? I want everybody to be happy, yet no matter which one I choose, somebody is not going to be pleased. I am not really a good athlete. When I think about soccer my stomach starts doing flips. I am not really a talented musician. When I think about playing the drums, my jaws start clenching. But I am really a good RILEE bear. I love people. At the neighborhood camp, I will be able to have fun being a good friend. That is what I do best, and that is what I will choose. It is okay to be the best RILEE bear I can be. Maybe my dad will be okay with this if I try a little harder to be physically fit. And maybe my mom would be okay with this if I try a little harder to get some rhythm. Maybe I can lose a little weight and swing a little more. Then everybody will be happy. But what I really want is for Mom and Dad to see me, the RILEE bear, not me the soccer bear or me the drummer bear." Here are the RILEE bear's FACTS:

FACTS	Soccer Camp		Music Camp		Neighborhood Camp	
	Pros	*Cons*	*Pros*	*Cons*	*Pros*	*Cons*
Feeling	—	It's scary	—	It's scary	It's comfy.	—
Thinking	—	What if I fail?	—	This is too hard.	This is familiar.	—
Sensing	—	My stomach is flipping.	—	My jaws are clenching.	I feel calm.	—
Acting	It pleases Dad.	Mom and I aren't pleased.	It pleases Mom.	Dad and I aren't pleased.	It pleases me.	Mom and Dad aren't pleased.
Choosing	It works for Dad.	It won't work for Mom.	It works for Mom.	It won't work for Dad.	It works for me.	It's the same as now.

Now it's time for you to write about one of your own experiences with making a difficult choice. Please use extra paper so that every member of your family can participate. List possible choices below (or on another piece of paper).

1. _____

2. _____

3. _____

Now examine your choices by finding the facts. Remember, it is your job to consider all the FACTS before making a decision. When you present the FACTS, it is possible for you and your family to discuss even the most difficult subjects without fear of rejection or disapproval. Bringing all the FACTS into a family discussion sets the tone for mutual respect and compromise.

Remember that you have to find a way that your family can be okay with your choice. Because that's what being a part of a family is all about. So what did you choose?

FACTS	Choice 1		Choice 2		Choice 3	
	Pros	Cons	Pros	Cons	Pros	Cons
Feeling						
Thinking						
Sensing						
Acting						
Choosing						

Now that you know how to understand the FACTS and make healthy choices, let's play the RILEE Bear FACTS Game.

 # RILEE Bear FACTS Game

The purpose of the RILEE Bear FACTS Game is to further help you create a healthy RILEE family. You have learned about how FAT can be restructured by recognizing that all family emotions operate on a continuum. It is time to operate in the middle of the continuum instead of at one extreme or the other.

Directions: Pick a comfortable area with good lighting. You will need a pair of dice. You will notice that each "stone" in the illustration has a letter on it, either "F" for feeling, "A" for acting, "C" for choosing, "T" for thinking, or "S" for sensing. First, color the stones going to each room according to the following:

Work room—F=Red; A=Red; C=Black; T=Green; and S=Yellow

Family room—F=Yellow; A=Yellow; C=Black; T=Green; and S=Red

Play room—F=Green; A=Green; C=Black; T=Red; and S=Yellow

All-purpose room—F=Black; A=Yellow; C=Black; T=Red; and S=Green

The goal of the game is to land in the room of your choice, but to get there, you have to consider the FACTS en route. The colors represent choices you can make to either *stop* the family from progressing (*red* is for stopper), *keep* the family in neutral (*yellow*), or *help* the family move forward (*green*).

Everyone begins at RILEE Bear in the middle. Each family member rolls the dice, and whoever gets the highest roll gets to move one stone toward the room of his or her choice. The player with the second highest roll moves one stone toward a different room, and so on. The first player then rolls the dice to begin again, and everyone plays until you've landed in the rooms of your choice.

As each player progresses toward a room, you should read the scenario to that room out loud. Invite family members to answer and discuss the scenario for each room, based on the color and letter of the stone on which the player landed. Remember, *red* generates a stopper response, yellow a neutral response, and *green* a helper response. If you landed on an "F" and it is red, you are to use a *stopper feeling*. If you landed on an "A" and it is yellow, you are to take a *neutral action*. And so forth. Black stones are used as wild cards. The family member who lands on a black stone can use any one of the three choices (stopper, neutral, helper). Explore all the color choices and different FACTS. Which combinations move things forward, and which ones hold things back?

Work Room
School/Job

Family Room
Family/Friends

F

S

A

T

C

C

T

A

S

F

RILEE BEAR FACTS FINDER

S

F

T

A

C

C

A

T

F

S

Play Room
Fun/Sports

**All-Purpose
Room**
Situations/
Problems

Here are the scenarios. Write your responses in the space provided.

The work room. You are doing your homework at the desk, but your mother needs the desk to balance the checkbook and pay bills. What do you do?

_____

_____

_____

_____

_____

The family room. You have a friend visiting in the family room. So does your dad. Your dad is discussing an upcoming hunting trip with his friend, but you and your friend want to watch your favorite television program on the big screen TV. What do you do?

_____

_____

_____

_____

_____

The playroom. You have been playing in the playroom all day, and it is a mess! Your parents have told you that you have to clean the room before you may go to a 7:00 P.M. movie with a friend. It is 6:30 P.M. You don't have time to do a good job. What do you do?

_____

_____

_____

_____

The all-purpose room. You just broke your grandmother's favorite lamp. She always talks about how irreplaceable it is. No one really saw you do it. What do you do?

_____

_____

_____

_____

_____

_____

FACTS vs. FATs

Did you notice that FACTS (feeling, acting, choosing, thinking, sensing) and FATs (family affective themes) look a lot alike? When your family affective themes come up, there is no "C" for choosing; you're just reacting the old way. Remember, *choices* keep you in the here and now; whereas, reactions take you back in time, often to a time when you felt hurt. (Note to parents: You will need to briefly explain to your children the content of chapter 3, where family affective themes [FATs] were discussed.) Family affective themes produce stopper reactions. Therefore, they need to be identified, labeled, and shared so that they can be put to rest and become just a part of your history, not your entire story. Therefore, it is important that you think about your family affective themes and discuss them with your family.

When you study history, you read about people and their countries. Usually, countries have symbols that are unique to them. So do people. When you think about the country of Ireland, a four leaf clover may come to mind. Likewise, when you think about your favorite athlete, the number on his or her uniform may pop into your head. It is good to understand how symbols become attached to countries and people. See what you can learn from the next exercise.

Exercise 5.2 Nations FLAGS

In school, kids study about the flags of different nations and what they mean. Together, in this exercise, match the right flag to the right description. Do so by drawing lines between the flags and their countries. Imagine how these flags would look if they were in bright colors.

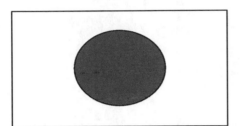

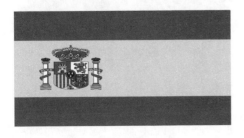

The **Brazilian Flag** is composed of green and yellow, a celestial sphere and a white band with words.

The yellow and green refer to the royal houses. The sphere is a portrait of the sky, and the words stand for order and progress.

The **Spanish Flag** is composed of red and yellow with Spain's coat of arms.

The colors were decided by a contest and are consistent with the colors of

---

The **American Flag** is composed of thirteen red and white stripes and fifty stars on a blue background.

The stripes stand for the original thirteen colonies and the stars represent the fifty states. Red signifies valor, white indicates purity, and

---

The **Japanese Flag** is composed of a red sun on a white field.

It signifies the country's name, *Nippon* or *Nihon*, meaning "Source of the Sun" or "Land of the Rising Sun."

The **Kenyan Flag** is composed of black, red, and green colors with a shield and two spears.

The color black represents majority, red indicates blood, and green signifies natural wealth. The white symbolizes peace, and the shield and two spears symbolize freedom.

Imagining is sometimes a lot more fun than remembering. In dealing with your FATs, you might have to remember feelings that you would rather forget. It would be nice if all feelings were like four leaf clovers, but many are not. Those feelings are the FATs you have to face. In this exercise, RILEE Bear will help you face those FATs feelings.

Exercise 5.3 Your FATs Feeling Flag

Now, parents and children, it's time for you to think about your own flags. You know, your own FATs feeling flag. RILEE Bear goes first. He chooses the number 6.

A. Please circle your most familiar FAT feeling:

  1. scary

  2. angry

  3. anxious

  4. embarrassed

  5. sad

  6. happy

B. Next circle its companion feeling. It will be the same number as above. Again RILEE Bear will choose number 6. What will you circle?

  1. comfy

  2. friendly

  3. calm

  4. proud

  5. glad

  6. gloomy

C. Finally, select a desired behavior, the behavior (action) you want to exercise. RILEE bear chooses 6. What will you circle?

  1. secure attachment

  2. attention

  3. acceptance

  4. approval

  5. acknowledgement

  6. affection

RILEE Bear has labeled his FATs feeling flag. Would you please color it for him? Now, you and your family are invited to label and color your own flags, whatever colors you would like.

RILEE's Flag   **Your Flag**

a Happy   a
       (Pink)
                    c Affection   c
b Gloomy
       (Brown)   (Yellow)   b

Now that all of the components of your flag have been properly identified and labeled, you can share them. What do the words mean to you?

Words | **Meaning**

_____ | _____

_____ | _____

_____ | _____

What do the colors mean to you?

Colors | **Meaning**

_____ | _____

_____ | _____

_____ | _____

Now share an experience that tells about your old (trait) FATs feeling flag. How does it feel to share your story?

_____

_____

_____

Do you know how to change your old trait FATs feeling flag into a new state FATs feeling flag? The easiest way is to increase the size of the desired behavior you want to exercise. Do it. Color it. Please remember to color RILEE's state flag as well.

RILEE's Flag   **Your Flag**

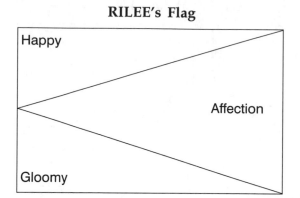
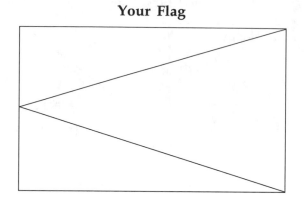

RILEE Bear can tell you that when he gets more affection, he can feel better, even in gloomy times. Does the change you made make you feel better? Perhaps not right away, but eventually it will. So keep waving your new flag.

Remember, changing the old trait FATs into the new state FATs is a matter of *choosing* (there's that word again!) healthy behaviors over and over again—good habits turn flab into muscle. So make a habit of both choosing and inviting these six healthy behaviors:

1. secure attachment

2. attention

3. acceptance

4. approval

5. acknowledgment

6. affection

But even when you change your old trait FATs flag into a new state FATs flag by changing your behaviors, you are still dealing with your history. It's time for a new chapter—the present. Every time you choose a healthy feeling, you choose the present.

Exercise 5.4 FACTS Feeling Flag

Now it's time for everyone in the family to choose the present by making their very own FACTS feeling flag. First, take a look at RILEE Bear's flag.

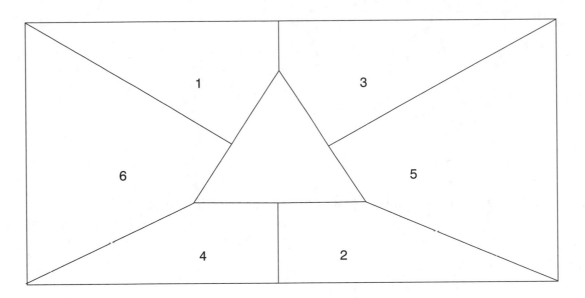

RILEE's Flag

These are the colors RILEE Bear chose: 1. orange, 2. red, 3. yellow, 4. purple, 5. green, 6. blue. Please color RILEE Bear's flag. These are the colors in a rainbow. When they are all combined together in the sunlight, they produce a most radiant white—a RILEE white, which is in the middle.

Now, work on your FACTS flag. Everyone in the family can make his or her own flag. First, choose one feeling from each line:

1. comfy or scary

2. angry or friendly

3. anxious or calm

4. embarrassed or proud

5. sad or glad

6. happy or gloomy

Second, choose one color for each feeling. Since the whole family is doing this, use additional pieces of paper to fill in the blanks, or photocopy the next pages, so each person can work on his or her own flag.

	Feeling	Color
1		
2		
3		
4		
5		
6		

Third, say what the colors you chose for each feeling mean to you.

	Feeling	Color
1		
2		
3		
4		
5		
6		

Now, put it all together.

"My FACTS flag is composed of _____

_____."

"It means _____

_____."

"It represents _____

_____."

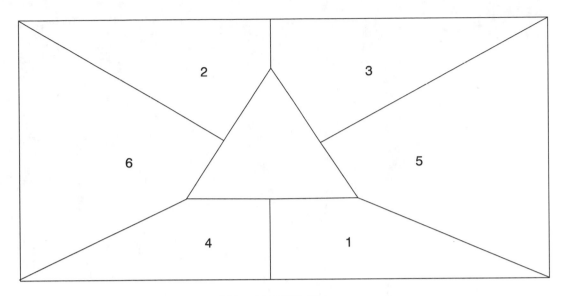

Your FACTS Flag

Congratulations! You've done it! You've identified your old trait FATs, made a new FATs state, and chosen a balanced FACTS flag. You've done it by choosing a new path, a balanced path that will serve you well. Close your eyes now. Imagine your FACTS flag waving in the breeze. Hold on to that image. In this way you can take it with you everywhere. Remember, keep the balance. Keep the C in your FACTS.

chapter 6

How Anger Works

Anger is a powerful negative expression of rage. It may be displayed in words and gestures ranging from mild displeasure to overt hostility. It significantly interferes with relating. Giving way to anger suggests a lack of mastery.

Four Stages of Anger

According to Murphy and Oberlin (2001), four stages of anger can be observed in children. Murphy and Oberlin refer to stage one as "the buildup" and state that "the buildup stage sets the foundation upon which the anger will be built. It is filled with memories of old unresolved conflicts, poor problem-solving skills, and stresses of the child's age and stage of development. Hours, days, even months of tension can accumulate until the angry child can no longer take it" (24).

Stage two is called "the spark," which is the action or thought that sets off the angry outburst. It may be big or small. It can be a thought, a feeling the child experiences, or an action by someone else. Kids respond differently to potential sparks. Some may react with rage, while some may have no reaction at all.

Stage three is identified as "the explosion." "This is the stage that gets all the attention—the one where the most meanness, aggression, and sometimes violence come to light. It's where feelings get hurt and property damaged. It's the explosion stage that most provokes parents to lose their temper and causes all of the peacemaking efforts to come crashing down" (33).

Stage four is called "the aftermath" which is "the most important stage in dealing with anger, and it's also the most overlooked. The aftermath is when parents and children can confront both the original problem along with any new ones that may have come from the explosion. Whether you've been through a minor skirmish or a major battle, there will be wounded feelings and other injuries to address. Take care of them now. Small outbursts almost inevitably will escalate to large ones if the underlying cause is ignored. Whatever is left unresolved becomes the build up for the next angry outburst" (37).

Prevention, diffusion, containment, and resolution are Murphy and Oberlin's suggested parental intervention goals for each respective stage. The intervention goal for the first stage, the buildup, is *prevention*; whereas the second stage, the spark, requires *diffusion*. In the third stage, the explosion, *containment* is the goal, and in the fourth stage, the aftermath, *resolution* is essential.

Prevention interventions include dealing with the child's immediate needs, avoiding unnecessary frustration, talking calmly, teaching problem-solving skills, and understanding your child's developmental level. Diffusion interventions include finding the true source of the problem, remaining calm, being a good listener, matching the face and the feeling, clarifying the rules, and offering a diversion. Containment interventions include cooling off, staying calm, separating entanglements, avoiding threats and bargaining, and restating disciplinary agreements. Resolution interventions include talking things out, teaching better problem-solving skills, managing outbursts before they escalate, having regular family meetings, and being consistent with discipline.

These interventions are quite compatible with those offered in this workbook. The major difference, however, is that in this workbook, *all* family members are encouraged to achieve the goal of personal intervention or personal mastery, whereas Murphy and Oberlin's focus is primarily on parental intervention.

One day RILEE Bear walked by a karate-dojo. *Dojo* is the Japanese word for school. He peeked in the window. All the bears were dressed in sparkling white uniforms and had rainbow-colored belts around their tummies. There were many white belts and yellow belts and gold belts and orange belts. Some bears wore blue belts or green belts or purple belts. A couple of bears wore brown belts. But one very special bear wore a beautiful black belt. He looked so handsome and calm. And you know what? He was the smallest bear there. Yet all the other bears looked up to him. RILEE Bear was impressed with the bear with the black belt. He wanted to be like him.

Goal: Achieve the Black Belt of Anger Mastery

The goal of this workbook is for all family members to master their own personal behaviors. Thus, all members of your family are encouraged to achieve the black belt of anger mastery, just like RILEE Bear. This is the highest level of anger mastery that can be obtained. Thus, a black belt is a symbol of worth and confidence that commands the esteem of others. With the exercises that follow, please photocopy the pages or use additional paper, so everyone can participate.

Exercise 6.1 "Me When I'm Angry"

Show your family how your face looks when you are angry. Use separate sheets of paper (white freezer paper works great) and either crayons or markers. Have all members of your family participate. Take some time. Notice what your eyes, eyebrows, nose, mouth, expression, and coloring look like when you are angry. Talk about it. Ask others if this is what they see. Now, as a family, draw what each of you looks like when angry. Draw your faces in the circles below. You can add more circles if needed.

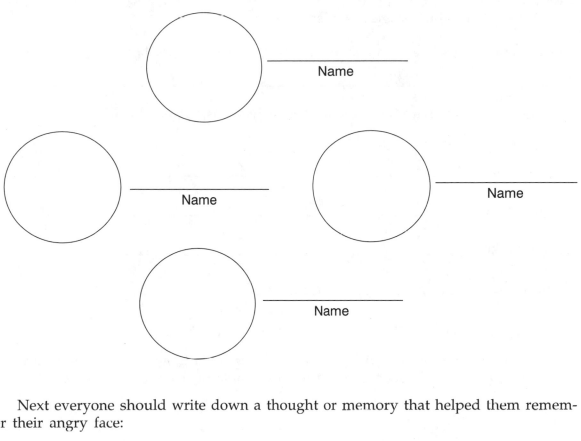

Next everyone should write down a thought or memory that helped them remember their angry face:

"The thought that made me angry was _____ _____

_____

_____."

"The memory that made me angry was _____

_____

_____."

Now, each of you should check which of Murphy and Oberlin's stages you are in when you finally show your angry face.

Your name: _____

   1. build up _____

   2. spark _____

   3. explosion _____

4. aftermath _____

Have other family members check to see if they agree. Would they say you were in a different stage? Talk about it.

Write down which stage is the scariest.

'The scariest angry stage for me in my family is number _____ because _____

_____."

Talk about this scary angry stage. What happens inside of you?

"When I am in this scary angry stage,

"I am *feeling* _____."

"I am *acting* _____."

"I am *thinking* _____."

"I am *sensing* _____."

Now turn these "FATS" into FACTS. Write down how you can do this.

When I am focusing on the FACTS, I am choosing good thoughts, healthy feelings and sensations, and positive actions. Here is an example of the FACTS I can create all by myself.

_____

_____

_____

_____

Good job! You are really beginning to understand how anger works. Now the RILEE Bear will help you with the next group of exercises. These are especially good to do with very young children, who can easily relate to RILEE Bear.

Exercise 6.2 Matching Faces and Feelings

The RILEE Bear wants to introduce you to six of his cousins. They are Happy Bear, Scared Bear, Sad Bear, Anxious Bear, Angry Bear, and Embarrassed Bear. Can you find them? Match the feeling to the picture by adding the correct number over the bear's forehead. Then draw a line from the name to the face.

For fun, first have the younger children in the family complete this exercise, and then have everyone else in the family complete it.

1. **Angry Bear**

\# _____

2. **Happy Bear**

\# _____

3. **Scared Bear**

\# _____

4. **Sad Bear**

\# _____

5. **Embarrassed Bear**

\# _____

6. **Anxious Bear**

\# _____

Answers: 1B, 2F, 3E, 4D, 5A, 6C

Exercise 6.3 Guess the Feeling

Now name the correct feeling in the blank space. Then look at the bears' faces below, and above each one's forehead, write the number of the scenario that matches the feelings expressed on the bear's face.

1. Tammy was getting on the school bus. She tripped and fell. The other kids laughed. Tammy felt _____.

2. Chun was home alone one night. It began to storm. The lights went out. Everything was really dark. Chun felt _____.

3. Billy lost his puppy last week. He still can't find him. He loves his puppy very much. Billy feels _____.

4. Mark thought he had done poorly on his math test. When he got his test back, he saw that he had made an A. Mark was very _____.

5. Margarita's dad asked her to sing for his parents. She was not prepared. Margarita felt _____.

6. Shenita took her brother's toy without asking. She broke it. When Daren found out, he was _____.

Good job! Now you know how to match six of the most important feelings to the way it looks on someone's face. But let's focus on the Angry Bear face. When do you become an angry bear? The next part of the workbook will help you to learn more about this.

Four Big Anger Sources

Consider four of the main sources of anger. It is easy to give in to angry feelings when these bears are around. They are always causing trouble. They are

1. Teaser Bear

2. Blamer Bear

3. Wanter Bear

4. Challenger Bear

Teaser Bear

Teaser Bear does really bad things. He has a way of telling you how he feels without having to take responsibility for what he says, what he does, or what gestures he makes. He puts you in a double bind box. He makes you feel bad. RILEE Bear often feels very paralyzed whenever he's around. Here is an example of what Teaser Bear does:

> Message 1: Rilee Bear, you look so fat in that blue sweater.
>
> Message 2: No you don't. I was just teasing.

Figure 6.1 Teasing Box

Exercise 6.4 Your Teasing Box

Write down your own example below. You know it well. It is the dual message that really gets to you whenever your own Teaser Bear is around.

Message 1: _____

_____

Message 2: _____

_____

Now, write down what you think and how you feel when you find yourself in this teasing box.

"I think _____

_____."

"I feel _____

_____."

After he says something very mean, Teaser Bear loves to say things like, "I was just teasing." "I was just kidding." "You know I didn't really mean that." "Can't you take a joke?" This way, he doesn't have to take responsibility for hurting your feelings. He uses these statements so that you can't express your anger. Have you noticed that, when your Teaser Bear does this, it really takes a toll on your self-esteem? Self-esteem is defined as the feelings and images, both positive and negative, that you have about yourself. Eventually these teaser messages lead to unexpected expressions of rage, for that is what happens when you cannot express your anger directly and appropriately. At such times, your anger will build up and come out like a tornado. Then you have created real trouble for yourself, and the cleanup is enormous!

Exercise 6.5 Understanding Teasing

You can prevent teasing through understanding. Have all members of your family participate and answer the following questions.

1. Do people tease you a lot? _____

_____

2. How do you feel when you are teased? _____

_____

3. What should you do the next time someone teases you? _____

_____

4. Do you tease other people a lot? _____

_____

5. When do you tease other people? _____

_____

6. How do you think other people feel when you tease them? _____

_____

7. When does Teaser Bear come out in your family? _____

_____

8. How does Teaser Bear behave? _____

_____

Exercise 6.6 Making Better Choices

Now let's see what you have learned. Can you respond with understanding and not let Teaser Bear win? Here are some examples. Read the following stories. Test yourself. What would you do in each case? What would the outcome be if you had to choose from the four choices listed below? For the purpose of this exercise, think of these as just choices, rather than right or wrong choices.

A. Reginald and Billy were playing football with some of the kids from school. Billy threw the ball to Reginald. Reginald caught the ball, and Billy shouted, "Well butter-fingers, you finally caught the ball!" Billy's teasing made Reginald angry. Reginald had four choices. What would the outcome be for each choice?

Choice	Outcome
1. Quit playing football.	
2. Start a fight with Billy.	
3. Ignore Billy's teasing and finish playing the game.	
4. Confront Billy with his teasing and leave.	

Note that choices 1, 2, and 4 will actually create more conflict, whereas choice 3 can lead to a sense of mastery.

B. Sarah had been working on her drawing for days. When she was finished, she showed it to Mary. Instead of saying something nice about the drawing, Mary laughed and told Sarah that it was the ugliest drawing she had ever seen. Mary also told Sarah that, since she was the teacher's pet, she would probably get an A anyway. Sarah felt very hurt. Sarah had four choices. What would the outcome be for each choice?

Choice	Outcome
1. Tell Mary that what she said was not okay.	
2. Throw her picture away.	
3. Ignore Mary's teasing and be proud of her work.	
4. Tell Mary that she is the one who is ugly.	

Note that choices 2 and 4 will actually create more conflict, whereas choices 1 and 3 can lead to a sense of mastery.

C. Paul went to the fair with his friends. Everyone got in line to ride the roller coaster, but Paul noticed a sign that said he was too short to ride. His friends teased him and called him "Pee Wee Pauly." This made Paul feel really sad. Paul had four choices. What would the outcome be for each choice?

Choice	Outcome
1. Call home and ask Mom to come and get him.	
2. Tell his friends to stop it and suggest that they all go find something else to do.	
3. Ignore his friends and go ride something else while they're on the roller coaster.	
4. Sneak onto the roller coaster when the person working the ride wasn't looking.	

Note that choices 1 and 4 will actually create more conflict, whereas choices 2 and 3 can lead to a sense of mastery.

Exercise 6.7 Remembering When

Think about a time when you became a teaser bear and teased a friend to make him or her feel bad. What was the outcome? Write your answers below.

"I remember when _____

_____

_____

_____."

"The outcome was _____

_____

_____

_____."

Contract 1: Make a Contract to Stop Teasing

As a part of being black belt masters in the making, all family members agree to *stop all teasing under all circumstances. No exceptions.*

Now color this stop sign red and sign below.

STOP
ALL
TEASING

We promise to say goodbye to Teaser Bear because he makes us feel bad about ourselves.

_____   _____
Signature   Signature

_____   _____
Signature   Signature

Blamer Bear

When RILEE Bear's cousin Blamer Bear comes to visit, he blames RILEE for things. When Blamer Bear doesn't like how things turn out, it is easier for him to think that it is RILEE Bear's fault. This allows him to be mad at someone else rather than himself. Here is an example. Blamer Bear knew that he was not allowed to throw a ball in the house, but he did it anyway. Blamer Bear threw the ball but RILEE Bear didn't catch it. The ball hit a vase and broke it. When RILEE's mom found out, Blamer Bear said that it was RILEE Bear's fault for not catching the ball. Instead of saying, "I'm sorry, I shouldn't have been throwing the ball in your house," he turned to RILEE and said, "If you had caught the ball, we wouldn't be in trouble." At that point, RILEE lost control and became a tornado, creating even more trouble for himself and his mom.

Exercise 6.8 Understanding Blaming

After many more tornados and hurt feelings, Rilee Bear decided to master the blamer bear part of himself. He achieved this by understanding what was going on. Then the blamer bear part of him no longer had so much power. You can diffuse blaming, too. Have all members of your family participate and answer the following questions.

1. Do people blame you a lot? _____

_____

2. How do you feel when you are blamed? _____

_____

3. What should you do the next time someone blames you? _____

_____

4. Do you blame other people a lot? _____

_____

5. When do you blame other people? _____

_____

6. How do you think other people feel when you blame them? _____

_____

7. When does Blamer Bear come out in your family? _____

_____

8. How does Blamer Bear behave? _____

_____

Exercise 6.9 Making Better Choices

Now let's see what you have learned. Can you respond with understanding and not let Blamer Bear win? Read the following stories and test yourself. What would you do if you were in each situation? What would the outcome be if you had to choose from the four choices listed below? Remember to think of these as just choices, rather than right or wrong choices.

A. Juan and Carlos were supposed to be at soccer practice at 5:00 P.M. Juan was still eating dinner when Carlos and his mom arrived to pick him up. Therefore, they were late for practice. When the coach asked why, Juan blamed Carlos for picking him up too late. Carlos was really angry. Carlos had four choices. What would the outcome be for each choice?

Choice	Outcome
1. Never pick Juan up for soccer practice again.	
2. Ignore what Juan said and practice.	
3. Tell Juan off and then tell his mother.	
4. Tell the coach his side of the story.	

Note that choices 1 and 3 will actually create more conflict, whereas choices 2 and 4 can lead to a sense of mastery.

B. Dominic and Gracie went shopping to buy their mom a birthday present. They had each saved five dollars for the present. The gift they selected was ten dollars, but the tax was ninety cents. They had forgotten about the tax. In front of the store clerk, Dominic blamed Gracie and said, "How could you be so dumb? You forgot about the tax. Now we won't be able to get Mom what she really wanted for her birthday." Gracie was very embarrassed. Gracie had four choices. What would the outcome be for each choice?

Choice	Outcome
1. Say nothing and select another present.	
2. Tell Dominic that it was his fault, too.	
3. Leave the store in tears.	
4. Suggest that they think of how to get ninety cents.	

Note that choices 1 and 3 will actually create more conflict, whereas choices 2 and 4 can lead to a sense of mastery.

C. Kisha and LaDonna were assigned to complete a school project together. Each girl was supposed to do one part at home. Then they were to meet Sunday afternoon to finish the project. It was due Monday. When Kisha arrived at LaDonna's house with her part completed, LaDonna had forgotten all about it, and she said, "Kisha, why didn't you call to remind me?" Kisha was very upset. Kisha had four choices. What would the outcome be for each choice?

Choice	Outcome
1. Tell LaDonna to stop blaming and do her part.	
2. Leave and tell the teacher that LaDonna forgot to do her part.	
3. Talk to LaDonna's parents to figure out what to do.	
4. Never speak to LaDonna again.	

Note that choices 2 and 4 will actually create more conflict, whereas choices 1 and 3 can lead to a sense of mastery.

Exercise 6.10 Remembering When

Think about a time when you became a blamer bear and blamed someone else for something you did. What was the outcome? Write you answers below.

"I remember when _____

_____

_____

_____."

"The outcome was _____

_____

_____

_____."

Contract 2: Make a Contract to Stop Blaming

As a part of being black belt masters in the making, all family members agree to *stop all blaming under all circumstances. No exceptions.*

Now, color this stop sign red and sign below.

We promise to say goodbye to Blamer Bear because he makes us feel bad about ourselves.

_____	_____
Signature	Signature
_____	_____
Signature	Signature

Wanter Bear

When RILEE Bear's cousin Wanter Bear comes to visit, she acts like a little princess. She believes that, because she wants something, she should have it. This is called *feeling entitled.* It means that because you believe you are special, you should always get your way, and you don't have to earn it. For example, sometimes you might believe that because you want something so much, no one should be able to tell you no. But that is not so. Not even royalty can always have their way, and neither can you.

The fact is that you can't always have everything you want. This is especially true when your excessive wanting hurts either you or other people. Sometimes this is hard to accept. For example, RILEE Bear sometimes wants to eat all the honey he can put in his mouth. But too much is not good for him. In fact, RILEE Bear usually wants more honey when he doesn't feel very good about himself. But, as we know, more is not necessarily better, and it certainly isn't a cure for low self-esteem.

Exercise 6.11 Understanding Excess Wanting

After wanting too much and paying too high a price for it, Rilee Bear decided to master the wanter bear part of himself. He achieved this by limiting his wants and not falling for his cousin's sense of entitlement. You can contain your own wants through understanding as well. Have all members of your family participate and answer the following questions.

1. How do you feel when you can't have something you want? _____

_____

2. What should you do the next time you don't get something you want? _____

_____

3. Do you purposely not let other people have the things they want? _____

_____

4. When do you deny other people the things they want? _____

_____

5. How do you think other people feel when you deny their requests? _____

_____

6. When does Wanter Bear come out in your family? _____

_____

7. How does Wanter Bear behave? _____

_____

Exercise 6.12 Making Better Choices

Now let's see what you have learned. Can you respond by understanding your needs and not letting Wanter Bear win? Read the following stories and test yourself. What would you do if you were in each situation? What would the outcome be if you had to choose from the four choices listed below? For the purpose of this exercise, think of these as just choices, rather than right or wrong choices.

A. Qwin and JoAnna were going to the mall with their moms. They were shopping for new party dresses. Qwin's mom was on a tight budget and told her what she could spend. JoAnna's mom was able to afford a more expensive dress. Qwin wanted the same dress that JoAnna picked. Her mom couldn't afford it. Qwin was really mad. She had four choices. What would the outcome be for each choice?

Choice	Outcome
1. Throw a tantrum and embarrass her mom.	
2. Try to find something similar in her price range.	

3. Become jealous of JoAnna and say unkind things to her.	
4. Refuse to buy any dress except the one JoAnna selected.	

Note that choices 1, 3, and 4 will actually create more conflict, whereas choice 2 can lead to a sense of mastery.

B. Ed joined Bobby's softball team. Bobby's dad was the coach. Ed was a good pitcher. Bobby was not. Bobby wanted to pitch, no matter what. The team was losing because Bobby was giving up too many runs. But Bobby insisted on finishing. The game was tied, and Bobby was pitching. Ed became very anxious. He had four choices. What would be the outcome for each choice?

Choice	Outcome
1. Say nothing to Bobby's dad (but talk about Bobby to all the other players).	
2. Ask Bobby's dad to call a time-out so that Bobby can settle down.	
3. Tell Bobby's dad that he (Ed) is a pretty good pitcher and ask to be put in the game.	
4. Decide not to play on Bobby's team anymore.	

Note that choices 1 and 4 will actually create more conflict, whereas choices 2 and 3 can lead to a sense of mastery.

C. Michelle and Jeremy were drawing. Jeremy wanted all of the primary colored markers, leaving Michelle with only the pastels. Michelle wanted to draw a picture of a forest and needed the strong browns and greens and blues; but Jeremy said no. Michelle felt very sad. Michelle had four choices. What would the outcome be for each choice?

Choice	Outcome
1. Do the best she could with the pastel markers.	
2. Go get Jeremy's aunt and tell on him.	
3. Tell Jeremy off and refuse to draw with him anymore.	
4. Dissolve into tears.	

Note that choices 2, 3, and 4 will actually create more conflict, whereas choice 1 can lead to a sense of mastery.

Exercise 6.13 Remembering When

Think about a time when you became a wanter bear and got angry because you couldn't have something you really wanted. What was the outcome? Write your answers below.

"I remember when _____

_____

_____

_____."

"The outcome was _____

_____

_____

_____."

Contract 3: Make a Contract to Stop the Excess Wanting

As part of being black belt masters in the making, all family members agree to *stop all excess wanting under all circumstances. No exceptions.*

Now, color the stop sign red and sign below.

STOP
ALL
EXCESS
WANTING

We promise to say goodbye to Wanter Bear because she makes us feel bad and sad about ourselves.

_____   _____
Signature   Signature

_____   _____
Signature   Signature

Challenger Bear

When RILEE Bear's cousin Challenger Bear comes to visit, she always challenges us when she doesn't get her way. Her favorite thing to say is "That's not fair." She gets angry because she believes that things should always be "fair," and fair means *her way*. But RILEE Bear has learned that what is fair for her may not be fair for him or someone else. For example, one day Challenger Bear wanted to go to the movies with RILEE. Her dad told her that she could only go after she cleaned up her room. She thought this was unfair. She called RILEE and found out that he didn't have to clean up his room before going to the movies. She again challenged her dad by telling him that his decision wasn't fair because RILEE Bear didn't have to clean up his room. Then Challenger Bear's dad called RILEE's mom, so RILEE had to clean up his room. RILEE Bear got really angry, and when he lost control of his anger, he got in trouble with his mom.

Exercise 6.14 Understanding Selfish Challenging

After challenging others to get his own way, RILEE Bear decided to master the challenger bear part of himself. He resolved this problem by dropping the words "fair" and "unfair" from his list of favorite words. You can do this, too. Have all members of your family participate and answer the following questions.

1. Do people often tell you that what you did is not fair? _____

   _____

2. How do you feel when you are told this? _____

   _____

3. What should you do the next time someone tells you this? _____

   _____

4. Do you often tell other people that what they want is not fair? _____

   _____

5. When do you tell other people this? _____

   _____

6. How do you think other people feel when you tell them this? _____

   _____

7. When does Challenger Bear come out in your family? _____

   _____

8. How does Challenger Bear behave? _____

_____

Exercise 6.15 Making Better Choices

Now let's see what you have learned. Can you respond by understanding and not letting Challenger Bear win? Read the following stories and test yourself. What would you do if you were in each situation? What would the outcome be if you had to choose from the four choices listed below? Remember to think of these as just choices, rather than right or wrong choices.

A. Brandon and Tommy were both A students, but only one person could go to district competition in math. Since Brandon went to the competition the previous year, Ms. Williams chose Tommy to go this year. Brandon was sad and mad and still wanted to go. He had four choices. What would the outcome be for each choice?

Choice	Outcome
1. Spread a rumor that Tommy cheated on his tests.	
2. Tell Ms. Williams how upset he is about how she chose Tommy. Ask if they could draw numbers.	
3. Talk to his friend, Derek, about how he wanted to go again because he had so much fun last year.	
4. To get back at Ms. Williams for not choosing him, start flunking his math tests purposely.	

Note that choices 1 and 4 will actually create more conflict, whereas choices 2 and 3 can lead to a sense of mastery.

B. Sarah wanted to go the Halloween party, but her parents would not allow her to stay out late on a school night. She would miss getting to go in the haunted house. Sarah was mad that she could not stay at the party longer and tried to convince her parents to let her stay by telling them how unfair they were. They did not change their mind. Sarah had four choices. What would the outcome be for each choice?

Choice	Outcome
1. Go in the haunted house anyway and make her parents wait for her to come out.	
2. Try to negotiate with her parents to allow her to stay just long enough to go in the haunted house.	

3. Yell and cry because she did not get her way.	
4. Talk to her parents about how angry she is but respect their rules.	

Note that choices 1 and 3 will actually create more conflict, whereas choices 2 and 4 can lead to a sense of mastery.

C. Karla had to wait until she was thirteen to get her ears pierced, but her younger sister Kim got hers pierced when she was eleven, after their parents divorced. Karla was furious. She had four choices. What would the outcome be for each choice?

Choice	Outcome
1. Not speak to her parents or Kim to "punish" them.	
2. Take all of Kim's earrings and hide them.	
3. Talk to her parents about her feelings.	
4. Talk to her best friend, Jessica, about how angry she is at her parents.	

Note that choices 1 and 2 will actually create more conflict, whereas choices 3 and 4 can lead to a sense of mastery.

Exercise 6.16 Remembering When

Remember a time when you thought someone was being unfair and you became a challenger bear. What did you do? What was the outcome? Write your answers below.

"I remember when _____

_____

_____

_____."

"The outcome was _____

_____

_____

_____."

Simply stated, telling someone something is "unfair" is an easy way to try to make others feel bad. In fact, this challenging of fairness is just a way to get your own way.

Contract 4: Make a Contract to Stop Fairness Challenging

As a part of being black belt masters in the making, all family members agree to *stop all fairness challenging under all circumstances. No exceptions.*

Now color the stop sign red and sign below.

STOP
ALL
FAIRNESS
CHALLENGING

We promise to say goodbye to Challenger Bear and her special words, "fair" and "unfair," because they make us feel angry.

_____   _____
Signature   Signature

_____   _____
Signature   Signature

The RILEE Path

The teaser bear, blamer bear, wanter bear, and challenger bear parts of you make others feel bad. These behaviors take you down the angry path. This was outlined in chapter 1, but in case you missed it, here it is again:

Angry path = rude and abusive behavior → disrespect → distrust → distress → hate.

It is much, much better to go down the RILEE path.

RILEE path = polite and courteous behavior → respect → trust → comfort → love.

But how can you keep on the RILEE path? You can turn to karate dō for help! This is what RILEE Bear did.

Karate-Dō

When RILEE bear started down the angry path, he got scared. He quickly figured out that there would always be a bigger, smarter, more powerful bear just around the corner. RILEE Bear was not really a clench-fisted bear. He was a RILEE Bear. Still he needed some help finding the RILEE path.

Remember when RILEE Bear walked by that karate-dojo? Remember how impressed he was with that bear with the black belt? Well, RILEE Bear decide to go in because he wanted what the black belt bear had: respect! And RILEE Bear knew that being angry was not the path he wanted to follow.

Hassell and Otis (2000) write about *karate-dō*. "Kara" means "empty," "te" means "hand," and "dō" means "path." Karate-dō teaches that anger blinds your choices and leads you to defeat if you let it be the master. When RILEE Bear heard about this, he knew immediately that he must follow the path of the open hand. No more clenched fists!

The karate path encouraged him to master his anger by dealing with the things that made him anxious. He practiced relaxing. You can, too.

Exercise 6.17 RILEE Relaxation

Directions: Parents, read the following exercise aloud while your children lie comfortably with room to move. Let them act out what the exercise tells them.

Hi, I am RILEE, the Re-lax-a-tion
Bear. When I was a Bear-in-the Box,
I often felt
scared,
and angry,
and anxious.
And I had to learn to deal
with these very upsetting feelings.
I tried all kinds of ways.

First, I tried to huff and puff and blow
the
box down.
That didn't work.
Then I tried to shout and scream
and throw temper tantrums.
That didn't work either.

One day, after exhausting myself,
I began to relax and
allow myself to calm down.
That worked!
Since it worked for me,
I know it will work for you.

So, lie down,
With your back on the ground,
wrinkle your nose,
wiggle your toes,
and tell yourself,

**"I can be comfy and safe,
any time, any place."**

When you tell yourself
"to be comfy and safe,
any time, any place,"
you will notice a big smile on your lips,
and a twinkle in your eyes;
then you will begin
to calm yourself down.

I was so overjoyed when I learned that
I, RILEE Bear,
could actually calm myself down.
I thought I needed my mom or my dad
or my grandma to do this for me.
But I was wrong.
I learned to do this for myself
and so can you!

It came to me, like a bolt out of the blue,
that whenever something happened,
I could choose what I thought about it.
Imagine that!
I could actually choose my thoughts!
And so can you.

Wow! What a great idea!
So when something happens,
or when you feel scared
or angry
or nervous inside,
I want you to tell yourself,

**"I can be comfy and safe,
any time, any place."**

Then I want you to put
a big smile on your lips,
and a twinkle in your eyes;
and notice your breathing.
When you think you are safe,
you will feel safe.
When you feel safe.
you will be safe.
You will begin to relax
and breathe deeply.
You will feel comfy,
Very, very comfy,
Very, very relaxed.

Notice how your toes tingle
When you relax and breathe deeply.
Notice how your chest goes
in and out, up and down
Just like a clown.

Now on the count of three,
I want you to make a clown face.
Here's how.
I want you to take a deep, deep breath
and fill up your cheeks with air,
So you look just like a clown
with big red cheeks.
Now hold that air in your cheeks
until I count to ten.
Then let it out slowly, and do it again.

Are you ready?
One-
Two-
Three-
Breathe deep, deep, deep.
Now, hold that breath in your cheeks
and use your fingers to count to ten.
One, two, three, four, five, six, seven,
eight, nine, ten.

Let that breath out slowly,
very, very slowly.
That's right!
Now do it again—
Are you ready?
One-
Two-
Three-
Breathe deep, deep, deep.
Now, hold that breath in your cheeks
and use your fingers to count to ten:
One, two, three, four, five, six, seven,
eight, nine, ten.

That's right, you did it!
Notice how all those
scary, anxious, and angry feelings
go away,
when you breathe deeply
and tell yourself

**that you
can keep yourself
comfy and safe,
any time, any place.**

How wonderful it is to know that you can
choose what you think
and how you feel.
Yes, you can comfort yourself just by
breathing deeply,
by breathing in
those cool safe feelings,
and breathing out
those hot, scary feelings.

Now you know that,
by breathing deeply and slowly
and by choosing good thoughts,

**you can feel calm and comfy and safe
any time and any place!**

That's great!
So, now let's do the opposite.
Here's your chance to practice being
really, really upset.
Remember the last time something
scared you, and you ran and
ran to get away.
Remember how you stopped because
you were so exhausted.
Remember you were
panting, panting, panting.

I remember it well ... You see,
I had climbed a tree

in search of a honey bee nest ...
I put my paw in the nest,
but out came the bees ...
Well, I never ran so fast in my life ...
I climbed down the tree,
scampered across the field,
and plunged into the pond ...
To get away from those very angry bees.

I noticed that my heart was pounding,
my breathing was shallow,
and I was panting, panting, panting.
I put my paw in front of my mouth.
My breath was so hot
I thought I was on fire.

So let's pretend that you, like me, are a
honey bear ...
climbing **up, up, up** the tree,
sticking your paw **in, in, in** the nest,
getting **bit, bit, bit** by the bees,
scampering **down, down, down** the tree,
running **across, across, across**
the meadow.
Diving **deep, deep, deep** into the pond,

panting **hot, hot, hot** air
from your chest onto your paw.

You see how easy it is to make yourself
scared, or angry, or anxious—
and it was all your imagination!
Or should I say it was my imagination.
You see, the thoughts can either come
from inside of you
or from outside of you.
So next time you go to a scary movie
notice how it works.
Notice the choices you make. Notice
how easy it is to make yourself
scared, or angry, or anxious.

But for now, breathe deeply,
put a smile on your lips
and a twinkle in your eye
and tell yourself,

**"I can feel comfy and safe,
any time, any place,**

just like my friend RILEE Bear."
Good job!

It feels so good to be relaxed—to leave those scary, angry, anxious feelings behind. Remember, you can do this any time, any place. Just read this exercise again or, even better, have someone read it to you so that you can just close your eyes and imagine. Remember to relieve your stress by relaxing whenever you can. That's what RILEE bears do.

Stress → Anxiety → Pain → Anger

The karate book (Hassell and Otis 2001) talks about how stress can actually weigh you down and cause you anxiety. Then, anxiety can cause pain. Since pain can turn to anger, it's important to always remember the RILEE path.

RILEE path = polite and courteous behavior → respect → trust → comfort → love.

But karate has a path, too (Hassell and Otis 2001), and it is a very good path:

Karate path: formal behavior → best effort → serenity → character.

You see how similar these two paths are! The RILEE path and the karate path have a principle in common: *Acting on anger is not okay*. So we have developed this RILEE Karate Game to help you develop your anger management skills.

RILEE Karate Game

Directions: To play this game, you will need some karate belts and a single die to roll. Cut and color some paper strips white, orange, purple, green, brown, and black, to use as belts. Each person rolls the die to determine his or her color: If you roll a one, you're white; a two, you're orange; a three, you're purple; a four, you're green; a five, you're brown. If you roll a six, you wear the black belt. White and orange are beginner belts. Purple and green are intermediate belts. Brown is an advanced belt. Black is the master/coach's belt. Make sure everyone has a different colored belt before you begin.

Contestants

White (1)

Orange (2)

Purple (3)

Green (4)

Brown (5)

Black/coach (6)

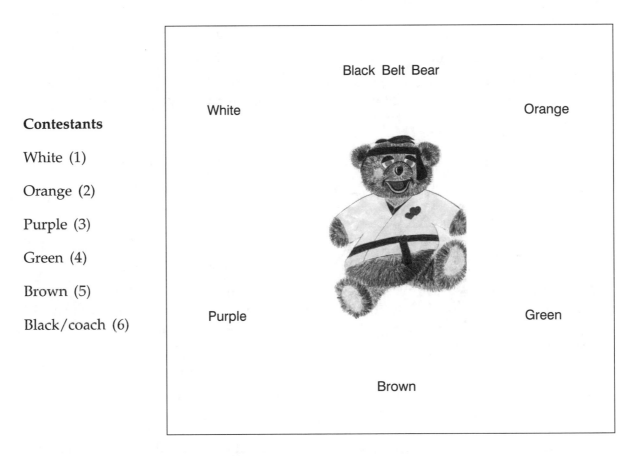

Now, look at the situation cards on the next page. Color them in and cut along the dotted lines. Pick the two cards that match your color. Everyone gets to respond to his or her situations. Roll the die again to determine who will go first. When you discuss the situation on your card, talk about something similar that happened to you. Remember to act out your response to the situation on the card. Respond according to your color and level of mastery.

RILEE Karate Situation Cards

(leave me white) You are talking to someone and that person doesn't answer you.	(leave me white) Your brother or sister takes one of your toys without asking.
(color me orange) You are being teased by your friends.	(color me orange) Someone makes a mistake and blames you for it.
(color me purple) Your parents punished you for not doing what you were told.	(color me purple) You lend one of your friends $2 and your friend won't pay you back.
(color me green) Your teacher gives you homework to do over the weekend.	(color me green) You can't find your new basketball.
(color me brown) Your little sister messes up your room, but your father makes you clean it up.	(color me brown) Everyone in the class was talking, but you were the only one who was sent to the principal's office.
(color me black) Your brother refuses to do what you want him to do.	(color me black) You said no to your friend and she challenged your decision.

Include the following behaviors in your responses.

Beginner Behaviors (white/orange)

* Disrespectful behavior
* Good effort
* Lack of serenity
* Weak character

Intermediate Behaviors (purple/green)

* Formal behavior
* Good effort
* Lack of serenity
* Weak character

Advanced Behaviors (brown)

* Formal behavior

* Best effort

* Lack of serenity

* Strong character

Master Behaviors (black)

* Formal behavior

* Best effort

* Serenity

* Strong character

Before you begin, there is one more important part to this RILEE Karate Game. You get to kick, punch, and shout! Yes, it's karate, so you get to choose your response, but you must follow these rules.

* A beginner can kick, but only if you can do so without anger and without contact. Contact means no touching, breaking, or striking.

* An intermediate player can punch, but only if you can do so without anger and without hurting anyone or anything. You can, however, use an old pillow.

* An advanced belt can shout, but only if you can do so without anger and without using bad language. Remember the family contracts you made. No teasing, blaming, excess wanting, or fairness challenging is allowed.

* A black belt displays a commanding masterful presence based on the FACTS. You can do or say anything that shows self-mastery.

Congratulations! Now that you have learned how to take good care of yourself, how to avoid a negative reaction by choosing a positive response, it is time to take those well earned RILEE Karate belts and proceed to the next chapter. In Chapter 7, you will learn more about anger as a defense. Good work. You are a black belt master in the making.

chapter 7

How to Recognize Anger

Anger is a powerful feeling. When your body senses a problem, it begins to put you on red alert. This is an automatic physical process. If left unchecked, it leads to anger. Although it is predictable, being on red alert looks slightly different for everyone.

Warning Signs

Can you tell when you are on red alert? Choose from the following list of signs, and add a few of your personal favorites. Invite all members of your family to participate. The red alert signs are

flushing face	avoiding eye contact
sweating	squinting eyes
feeling hot	looking disgusted
staring intensely	breathing shallowly
tightening lips	_____
stiffening body	_____

Knowing when you are on red alert can help you manage your anger. Knowledge is power. Anger is power. But knowledge is clearly more powerful than anger if you use it to respond. Otherwise, the defense of anger prevails and you will react.

Anger Is a Defense

Anger works as a defense. In the short run, it is an effective stopper. It is a good weapon. It makes you feel very powerful. That is why Teaser Bear, Blamer Bear, Wanter Bear, and Challenger Bear use it so often. But they hurt others when they react. In the long run, they also hurt themselves, and they damage their relationships.

Recognizing the Angry Child/Adult

According to Murphy and Oberlin (2001), the *angry child* has ten major defensive traits. He or she:

1. makes his/her own misery

2. cannot analyze problems

3. blames others for his/her misfortune

4. turns bad feelings into mad feelings

5. lacks empathy

6. attacks people rather than solves problems

7. uses anger to gain power

8. indulges in destructive self-talk

9. confuses anger with self-esteem

10. can be nice when he/she wants to be.

When these ten defenses are not recognized, labeled, and resolved, they move with us into adulthood. In order to help your children to address and resolve these defenses and to develop better coping strategies, you must first address these defenses within yourself.

Remember, a defense is a behavior that you use to cover up a vulnerable feeling or thought that is important to you. You want to protect it by diverting attention away from it. Just as athletes use defensive plays in order to keep the other team from scoring points, you may use anger to keep others from knowing how you really feel or what you really think. For example, sometimes you may say you are angry when you really are feeling hurt or lonely or sad or scared. These are very painful and vulnerable feelings. Anger is a diversion. It is a way of taking attention away from your painful and vulnerable feelings and turning the situation into something very different. That is what defensive football players do. They try to break up the play, get the offensive team off track, and create chaos. That is what anger does. It undermines effectiveness in you as well as others.

Returning to the "FATs"

Let's return to the FATs. We've talked about how FATs stands for *family affective themes*. We've also talked about FATs vs. FACTS. In terms of anger management, the terms FATS refers to *feeling, acting, thinking,* and *sensing*, without *choosing*. What you want to aim for, instead, is the FACTS. Do the following set of exercises with your family.

Feelings

Let's start with *feelings*: Do you wallow in your negative feelings? RILEE Bear's cousin Wallower Bear does. "Woe is me" is his main theme. He is always complaining. Nothing is ever right. Others are always doing him wrong. He is like a broken record. All he does is complain, complain, complain. When you try to help him fix his problems, it's like trying to contain a flood with a few Band-Aids. No matter what you do, Wallower Bear just finds a new problem to complain about. If you acknowledge his pain, he'll either stop or find someone else to listen to his tale of woes. Wallowing is a defense. It is very paralyzing. It is an effective smoke screen. The problem is that Wallower Bear doesn't know how to *communicate*.

Exercise 7.1 Understanding Wallowing

After many wallowing episodes, RILEE Bear decided to master the wallower bear part of himself. He achieved this by understanding what was going on. Then he stopped letting Wallower Bear complain. He did this by giving up his need to rescue Wallower Bear and to fix his problems. Then he didn't have so much power over RILEE Bear. You can *give up rescuing*, too. Answer the following questions.

1. Do people complain a lot to you? _____

_____

2. How do you feel when you have to listen to their tales of woe? _____

_____

3. What should you do the next time someone wants to dump all of their complaints on your shoulders? _____

_____

4. Do you complain a lot? _____

_____

5. When do you complain? _____

_____

6. How do you think other people feel when you complain? _____

_____

7. When does Wallower Bear come out in your family? _____

_____

8. How does Wallower Bear behave? _____

_____

Exercise 7.2 Making Better Choices

Now let's see what you have learned. Can you respond with understanding and not let Wallower Bear get to you? Here are some examples. Read the following stories. Test yourself. What would you do if you were in these situations? What would the outcome be if you had to choose from the four choices listed below? For the purpose of this exercise, think of these as just choices, rather than right or wrong choices.

A. Jamie and Marci were talking about their cheerleading tryouts. Neither girl made the squad. Jamie wanted to stop talking about their experiences and go on to planning the school party. But not Marci. She wanted to go on and on and on about it. She whined about her performance, she accused the judge of not liking her, she felt that she should have been given another chance to do the routine since she slipped and fell, and so on. Marci's wallowing made Jamie very tired. Jamie had four choices. What would the outcome be for each choice?

Choice	Outcome
1. Tell Marci to shut up.	
2. Tell Marci she should ask for another tryout.	
3. Ignore Marci's wallowing and start planning the party.	
4. Acknowledge Marci's pain.	

Note that choices 1, 2, and 3 will actually create more conflict, whereas choice 4 can lead to a sense of mastery.

B. Ronald stopped by to see Tommy because he was sick. Ronald had only a few minutes, but he wanted to check on his friend. He told Tommy that, but Tommy was so lonely he wouldn't let Ronald leave. Tommy went on and on about how sick he had been and how Ronald was the first classmate to come visit. He told Ronald every detail of his illness. Ronald was overwhelmed. He felt trapped. Ronald had four choices. What would the outcome be for each choice?

Choice	Outcome
1. Tell Tommy that he had to go and leave.	
2. Sit there and fume.	
3. Listen to Tommy's feelings.	
4. Run out and never talk to Tommy again.	

Note that choices 1, 2, and 4 will actually create more conflict, whereas choice 3 can lead to a sense of mastery.

C. John went to the ball game with Peter. A high fly ball was hit and the ball bounced through John's hands. Peter caught it. John spent the rest of the game complaining to Peter about his bad luck. Peter felt disgusted. Peter had four choices. What would the outcome be for each choice?

Choice	Outcome
1. Give John the ball.	
2. Tell John off.	
3. Get up and leave.	
4. Ask John if he was sad.	

Note that choices 2 and 3 will actually create more conflict, whereas choices 1 and 4 can lead to a sense of mastery.

Exercise 7.3 Remembering When

Think about a time when you became a wallower bear and complained and complained. What was the outcome?

"I remember when _____

_____

_____

_____."

"The outcome was _____

_____

_____

_____."

Contract 5: Make a Contract to Stop Wallowing

As a part of being a black belt masters in the making, all family members agree to *stop all wallowing under all circumstances. No exceptions.*

Now color this stop sign red and sign below.

STOP
ALL
WALLOWING

We promise to say goodbye to Wallower Bear because he makes us feel exhausted.

_____
Signature

_____
Signature

_____
Signature

_____
Signature

Acting

Do you act out your defenses? RILEE Bear's cousin Intruder Bear does. She is always in his face. She is so nice, so sickly sweet. She is always trying to get RILEE Bear to like her or accept her or include her. When she comes over, he wants to run for the hills. She is so intrusive. She has such low self-esteem that she is always trying to impress RILEE Bear. She has the best book or the most beautiful doll or the neatest game. It is so irritating. RILEE Bear learned that intruding is a defense. It is an effective way to run others off. Yet it is usually the opposite of what Intruder Bear really wants. She hates to be alone. The problem is that Intruder Bear doesn't know how to *relate*.

Exercise 7.4 Understanding Intruding

After many run-ins and angry feelings, RILEE Bear decided to master the intruder bear part of himself. He achieved this by understanding what was going on. Then Intruder Bear didn't have the power to upset him. When RILEE Bear realized that Intruder Bear was just trying to relate to him, he was able to show her ways that worked for him. When he gave up being angry with Intruder Bear, he didn't need to put up so many barriers. Then RILEE Bear began to feel better. You can give up building barriers and being angry, too.

1. Do people intrude on you a lot? _____

_____

2. How do you feel when they intrude? _____

_____

3. What should you do the next time someone is intrusive? _____

_____

4. Do you intrude on other people a lot? _____

_____

5. When do you intrude on other people? _____

_____

6. How do you think other people feel when you are intrusive? _____

_____

7. When does Intruder Bear come out in your family? _____

_____

8. How does Intruder Bear behave? _____

_____

Exercise 7.5 Making Better Choices

Now let's see what you have learned. Can you respond with understanding and not let Intruder Bear get to you? Here are some examples. Read the following stories. Test yourself. What would you do if you were in these situations? What would the outcome be if you had to choose from the four choices listed below? For the purpose of this exercise, think of these as just choices, rather than right or wrong choices.

A. Here comes Tammy. She wants to join Sonia and her friends for Sonia's first slumber party. Sonia is nine. Tammy is five; she is intruding. Sonia feels annoyed. Sonia had four choices. What would the outcome be for each choice?

Choice	Outcome
1. Call Mom to get Tammy.	
2. Lock Tammy out of the bedroom.	
3. Let Tammy stay for a little while.	
4. Yell and scream at Tammy and tell her to get lost.	

Note that choices 2 and 4 will actually create more conflict, whereas choices 1 and 3 can lead to a sense of mastery.

B. Karen is at the store. She is looking for a present for her dad. Her brother, Joey, wants to help, but Karen wants to do this all by herself. Karen feels pressured. Karen had four choices. What would the outcome be for each choice?

Choice	Outcome
1. Let Joey help.	
2. Call Mom to come get him.	
3. Yell at Joey and tell him to go away.	
4. Give Joey another task to do.	

Note that choice 3 will actually create more conflict, whereas choices 1, 2, and 4 can lead to a sense of mastery.

C. Eddie and Luke were eating breakfast. Luke kept trying to eat Eddie's cereal. Eddie was very annoyed. Eddie had four choices. What would the outcome be for each choice?

Choice	Outcome
1. Take Luke's spoon away and throw it on the floor.	
2. Ask Dad for help.	
3. Give Luke some of his cereal.	
4. Tell Luke to back off.	

Note that choices 1 and 4 will actually create more conflict, whereas choices 2 and 3 can lead to a sense of mastery.

Exercise 7.6 Remembering When

Think about a time when you became an intruder bear and wanted to feel secure and close. What was the outcome?

"I remember when _____

_____

_____."

"The outcome was _____

_____

_____."

Contract 6: Make a Contract to Stop Intruding

As a part of being a black belt masters in the making, all family members agree to *stop all intruding under all circumstances. No exceptions.*

Now color this stop sign red and sign below.

We promise to say goodbye to Intruder Bear because she makes us feel disgusted.

_____
Signature

_____
Signature

_____
Signature

_____
Signature

Thinking

Are you a good problem solver? Or do your thoughts often go round and round in circles? RILEE Bear's cousin Circular Bear never gets anywhere because the way she thinks doesn't make any sense. She repeats herself over and over and over. RILEE Bear gets so tired of listening to her. Remember the story of Chicken Little who got eaten by the fox? Well, that's RILEE's cousin. Her thinking is so circular and so repetitive. She never really listens to what anyone else says because she is so busy listening to herself. Listening to her is boring. RILEE Bear finally learned that this type of circular thinking is a defense. It is an effective way of getting others to not really listen to you. Yet it is usually used by those who want to be heard. The problem is that Circular Bear, herself, doesn't know how to *listen.*

Exercise 7.7 Understanding Circular Thinking

After many boring experiences, RILEE Bear decided to master the circular bear part of himself. He achieved this by understanding what was going on. Circular Bear was so afraid of not being heard that she never stopped talking. RILEE Bear could never get a word in edgewise. What to do? RILEE Bear finally learned to acknowledge Circular Bear's ideas and let her know the ideas that he really liked. Then Circular Bear didn't have the power to bore him. You can show interest, too. It's better than being bored or falling asleep.

1. Do people repeat themselves in front of you a lot? _____

_____

2. How do you feel when they go on and on and won't stop talking? _____

_____

3. What should you do the next time someone monopolizes the conversation?

_____

4. Do you repeat yourself a lot when you are with other people? _____

_____

5. When do you repeat yourself with other people? _____

_____

6. How do you think other people feel when you talk in circles? _____

_____

7. When does Circular Bear come out in your family? _____

_____

8. How does Circular Bear behave? _____

_____

Exercise 7.8 Making Better Choices

Now let's see what you have learned. Can you respond with understanding and not let Circular Bear get to you? Here are some examples. Read the following stories. Test yourself. What would you do if you were in these situations? What would the outcome be if you had to choose from the four choices listed below? For the purpose of this exercise, think of these as just choices, rather than right or wrong choices.

A. Jo Ellen and Stephanie were eating lunch together at school. Stephanie wanted to tell Jo Ellen about her new puppy, but she couldn't get a word in edgewise. Jo Ellen kept talking and talking and talking. Stephanie felt bored. Stephanie had four choices. What would the outcome be for each choice?

Choice	Outcome
1. Let Jo Ellen continue to talk.	
2. Cut Jo Ellen off and tell her about the puppy.	
3. Get up and join someone else.	

4. Ask Jo Ellen what is going on.	

Note that choices 2 and 3 will actually create more conflict, whereas choices 1 and 4 can lead to a sense of mastery.

B. Shaunda and Terrance were working in the yard raking leaves. Terrance complained constantly about having to do yard work. His complaining was making the task harder. Shaunda felt annoyed. Shaunda had four choices. What would the outcome be for each choice?

Choice	Outcome
1. Go tell Mom that Terrance is complaining.	
2. Start making fun of Terrance.	
3. Restate for Terrance what he is saying.	
4. Add more leaves for Terrance to rake.	

Note that choice 1, 2, and 4 will actually create more conflict, whereas choice 3 can lead to a sense of mastery.

C. Kim and Keri were talking with their teacher about their test scores. Both did well, but Kim thought she deserved an even higher grade. Kim tried continuously to get the teacher to change her grade. Keri felt embarrassed. Keri had four choices. What would the outcome be for each choice?

Choice	Outcome
1. Excuse herself and leave.	
2. Tell Kim to stop it.	
3. Acknowledge Kim's frustration.	
4. Ask for a better grade as well.	

Note that choice 4 will actually create more conflict, whereas choices 1, 2, and 3 can lead to a sense of mastery.

Exercise 7.9 Remembering When

Think about a time when you became a circular bear and repeated yourself over and over. What was the outcome?

"I remember when _____

_____

_____."

"The outcome was _____

_____

_____."

Contract 7: Make a Contract to Stop Circular Thinking

As a part of being a black belt masters in the making, all family members agree to *stop all circular thinking under all circumstances. No exceptions.*

Now color this stop sign red and sign below.

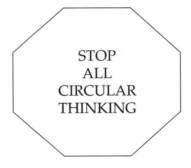

STOP
ALL
CIRCULAR
THINKING

We promise to say goodbye to Circular Bear because she makes us feel bored.

_____   _____
Signature   Signature

_____   _____
Signature   Signature

Sensing

Are you good at sensing a problem? Or do you just overreact? RILEE Bear's cousin Reactor Bear never gets anywhere. He makes so many mistakes. He doesn't even let others finish before he is interrupting and reacting. Usually his reactions are wrong. He is always misinterpreting others' behaviors or intentions. Being around him is exhausting. RILEE Bear eventually learned that this form of reacting is a defense. It is an effective way of not allowing others' input. Yet it is typically used by those who are highly anxious and need help with their choices. The problem is that Reactor Bear doesn't know how to *behave*.

Exercise 7.10 Understanding Overreacting

After many experiences with overreacting to get attention, RILEE Bear decided to master the reactor bear part of himself. He achieved this by understanding what was going on. Reactor Bear was so afraid of not getting enough attention that he behaved impulsively. He often made matters worse by jumping ahead before he considered the consequences of his behavior. He was always making messes. When RILEE Bear was with him, he was always getting into trouble. RILEE Bear finally learned to help Reactor Bear deal with his stress. He taught Reactor Bear his RILEE relaxation exercises. It worked. Now Reactor Bear knows how to behave and RILEE Bear can be calm rather than exhausted.

1. Do people often tell you that you are too impulsive? _____

_____

2. How do you feel when you are told this? _____

_____

3. What should you do the next time someone tells you that you overreacted?

_____

4. Do you often tell other people that they overreact or are impulsive? _____

_____

5. When do you overreact with other people? _____

_____

6. How do you think other people feel when you overreact or are impulsive?

_____

7. When does Reactor Bear come out in your family? _____

_____

8. How does Reactor Bear behave? _____

_____

Exercise 7.11 Making Better Choices

Now let's see what you have learned. Can you respond with understanding and not let Reactor Bear get to you? Here are some examples. Read the following stories. Test yourself. What would you do if you were in these situations? What would the outcome be if you had to choose from the four choices listed below? For the purpose of this exercise, think of these as just choices, rather than right or wrong choices.

A. Celia was waiting in line to buy movie tickets. Johnny broke into the line and insisted that Celia buy him a ticket. Celia said no, and Johnny reacted angrily to her. Celia felt upset. She had four choices. What would the outcome be for each choice?

Choice	Outcome
1. Push him out of the way.	
2. Nicely suggest that he go to the back of the line.	
3. Acknowledge his desire to get into the movies.	
4. Let him in the line.	

Note that choices 1 and 4 will actually create more conflict, whereas choices 2 and 3 can lead to a sense of mastery.

B. Johnny finally got up to the ticket window, but the last ticket had just been sold. Johnny lost it and said all kinds of bad words. His friend, Benjamin, was really embarrassed. Benjamin had four choices. What would the outcome be for each choice?

Choice	Outcome
1. Try to calm Johnny down.	
2. Apologize to the theatre employee for Johnny's behavior.	
3. Pretend he doesn't know Johnny.	
4. Say that he is just as frustrated as Johnny is.	

Note that choice 3 will actually create more conflict, whereas choices 1, 2, and 4 can lead to a sense of mastery.

C. Rosa and Monica were playing dolls. Rosa forgot that Monica's doll was supposed to be two, not eight. Monica jumped all over her for making a mistake. She was relentless. Rosa felt paralyzed. Rosa had four choices. What would the outcome be for each choice?

Choice	Outcome
1. Burst into tears.	
2. Ask Monica to back off.	
3. Leave and tell Monica's mom.	
4. Understand that Monica has a problem.	

Note that choices 1 and 3 will actually create more conflict, whereas choices 2 and 4 can lead to a sense of mastery.

Exercise 7.12 Remembering When

Think about a time when you became a reactor bear and either behaved impulsively and/or overreacted. What was the outcome?

"I remember when _____

_____

_____."

"The outcome was _____

_____

_____."

Contract 8: Make a Contract
to Stop Overreacting

As a part of being a black belt masters in the making, all family members agree to *stop all overreacting under all circumstances. No exceptions.*

Now color this stop sign red and sign below.

STOP
ALL
OVERREACTING

We promise to say goodbye to Reactor Bear because she makes us feel paralyzed.

Signature	Signature

Signature	Signature

Changing the FATs into FACTS

The difference between these FATs and FACTS is the C, which stands for *choosing*. Without the C, Wallower Bear, Intruder Bear, Circular Bear, and Reactor Bear are on the defense. They don't know how to *communicate, listen, relate,* and *behave*. They create chaos everywhere. If RILEE Bear let his cousins run the show, he would end up feeling para-lyzed, disgusted, bored, and exhausted. These are *not* RILEE feelings. They are angry, clench-fisted feelings. They are not good for RILEE, and they are not good for you.

RILEE Bear has learned that he can't be passive when his cousins Wallower Bear, Intruder Bear, Circular Bear, and Reactor Bear come to visit. He has to be active. He has to make good choices. He has to play offense and not allow their defense to dominate. He has to be aware when he goes on red alert, and he has to manage his FATs. This is a lot of work, but he remembers the lessons he learned from *karate-dō*, the karate path.

> Karate path: formal behavior → best effort → serenity → character.

When he returns to this path, he can free himself from his ten defensive traits. And so can you. The following RILEE relaxation exercise will show you how to get back on the right path.

Exercise 7.13 RILEE Relaxation

Directions: Parents, read the following exercise aloud while your children lie comfortably with room to move. Let them act out what the exercise tells them.

Here I am
Back again
I'm Rilee, the
Re-lax-a-tion Bear
Here to remind you
of all you learned in
the previous exercise.

Yes, you are on your way
to deep, deep, deep relaxation
Because you already know how to
wrinkle your nose,
wiggle you toes,
put a big smile on your lips
and a twinkle in you eye,
and say,
"I can be comfy and safe,
any time, any place."

Make this your special relaxation phrase,
your personal cue to relax.
It can work any time, any place.
All you have to do
is repeat it over and over again
until your fears disappear.

That's right, you can make your
fears appear or disappear.
It all depends
on what you choose to think
and how you choose to breathe.

Remember you learned this
in the previous exercise.
And now,
you will learn to relax all
your muscles

So, lie down,
with your back on the ground,
wrinkle your nose,
wiggle your toes,
and tell yourself,
"I can be comfy and safe,
any time, any place."
When you tell yourself
"to be comfy and safe,
any time, any place,"
you will notice
a big smile on you lips
and a twinkle in you eyes;
then you will begin
to calm yourself down.

Yes, relax and breathe deeply.
Notice how your toes tighten
Notice how your chest goes
in and out, up and down.
Breathe like a clown
Deep, deep, deep
down, down, down
Hold that breath in your cheeks
like a clown, clown, clown.

Notice how all your
scary, anxious, and angry feelings
go away
when you breathe deep, deep, deep
and tell yourself,
"I can be comfy and safe,
any time, any place."
Choose calm, calm thoughts
Choose cool, cool feelings
Choose smooth, smooth muscles.

Yes, you can choose to make your muscles
comfy and
smooth any time, any place.
You can relax your muscles by
Calming your thoughts
Cooling your feelings
and comforting your body.

Remember how very important your body is.
It senses when you are
scared, or angry, or anxious
It tightens up everywhere.
It puts you on "red alert"
automatically.
And before you know it,
you are all stiff and rigid.

If you hold
this body position for a long, long time,
you will overreact. Your body will act on
its red alert senses.
You will create trouble—
all because your body has
tightened up and put itself on red alert.
Choose to loosen up,
Choose comfy muscles,
Choose cool feelings,
Choose calm thoughts.

Remember: comfy muscles
cool feelings
calm thoughts.

Say, "I can feel comfy and safe,
any time, any place."

Then, practice letting your muscles go—
here's how.
Start with your face.
Think a scary thought,
Take a shallow breath,
Tighten all the muscles in your face and
jaw.
Make your angriest, angriest face
Hold you jaws tight, tight, tight!
Count to three.
One, two, three

Tight, tight, tight
four, five, six

Now . . .
Loose, loose, loose
Good.

Relax your face, drop your jaw,
think a calm thought,
take a deep breath,
let all your face
and jaw muscles go.
You did it. Good job!

Next, tighten all the muscles
in your hands . . . that's
right. Make two fists
Left fist, right fist
Now count to three
One, two, three
Tight, tight, tight!
Four, five, six.

Loose, loose, loose.
Good—relax your hands.

Shake your fingers,
Think a calm thought,
Take a deep breath,
Let your hands and fingers
go, go, go.
You did it! Good job.

Next, tighten all the muscles
In your shoulder . . . that's right,
shrug your shoulders
like you do when someone
asks you a question that you don't want to
answer.
And instead you scrunch up your shoulders
and say, "I don't know."

Do that now.
Shrug your shoulders . . . hold
them tight, tight, tight.
Count to three:
One, two, three
Tight, tight, tight!
Four, five, six
Say, "I don't know"

Now loose, loose, loose—
Let those shoulder muscles
go, go, go.
Think a calm thought
Take a deep breath
Let all of your shoulder muscles go limp.
You did it. Good job.

Next, with your heels still on the ground,
pull your toes forward as much as you can.
Hold them
tight, tight, tight.
Count to three:
One, two, three
tight, tight, tight!
four, five, six.

Loose, loose, loose.
Let those feet and leg muscles
go, go, go.

Think a calm thought,
Take a deep breath,
Let all of your feet and leg
muscles go, go, go.
Say, "I can keep myself
comfy and safe,
any time, any place.

Relax, relax, relax
breathe, breathe, breathe.
You did it. Good job.
Notice how easy it is to
relax your face, your
shoulders, your feet, your legs.
It's all about keeping
your thoughts calm,
your feelings cool,
and your body comfortable.
You can keep yourself
comfy and safe,
any time, any place.

Lastly, since I, RILEE Bear, am such
a good bench-warmer bear,
I often put my angry feelings
in my lower back muscles.
So, let's do one more
muscle relaxation exercise.

So, tighten up your stomach muscles
Pull your belly button
up, up, up.
Make your butt muscles
hard, hard, hard.
Hold it to a slow count of three.
One, two, three—
tight, tight, tight!
four, five, six.
Now, loose, loose, loose.

Let those stomach and butt
muscles
go, go, go.

Think a calm thought,
Take a deep breath,
Let all of you stomach and butt muscles
go, go, go.
You did it! Good job.

By relaxing your face and jaws
your shoulders,
your stomach, and your butt,
you can keep yourself comfy
and safe, any time, any place.
No matter what!

Remember to breathe
deep, deep, deep
down, down, down
hold that breath in your cheeks
like a clown, clown, clown.
Let that breath
out, out, out.

Now, tighten and relax your
jaw, jaw, jaw.
Tighten and relax your
shoulders, shoulders, shoulders.
Tighten and relax your
fist, fist, fist.
Tighten and relax your
feet, feet, feet.
Tighten and relax your
stomach, stomach, stomach.
Tighten and relax your
butt, butt, butt.
Say, "I can feel comfy and safe,
any time, any place."

Now you are truly becoming a
master in the making
for you can control the muscles in your
body.

Your body still does the sensing,
But you do the choosing.
You choose your responses.
You are choosing to be a
master in the making.

Congratulations, you are now a
master of the muscles.

It feels so good to relax your muscles, doesn't it? You can learn to relax whenever you need to relax. When you feel paralyzed, disgusted, bored, or exhausted, just relax your muscles. No more clenched fists!

Karate-Dō Lessons

It's time for more *karate-dō* lessons. Remember, the karate path requires a calm mind, stable feelings, the ability to sense trouble, and the self-discipline to act when no other choices are available. Can you see the RILEE path in those karate requirements?

RILEE path = polite and courteous behavior → respect → trust → comfort → love.

Now let's compare our synopsis of Murphy and Oberlin's angry traits (2001) with our synopsis of *karate-dō* traits. Which ones do you like better?

Angry Traits	RILEE's Karate-dō Traits
1. misery	1. joy
2. confusion	2. clarity
3. blaming	3. taking responsibility
4. turns bad feelings into mad feelings	4. turns bad feelings into good feelings
5. lacks empathy	5. has empathy
6. makes defensive choices	6. makes positive choices
7. enjoys power	7. enjoys relatedness
8. uses destructive self-talk	8. uses constructive self-talk
9. sees anger as mastery	9. sees balance as mastery
10. uses kindness to manipulate	10. uses kindness to relate

Remember, empathy is putting yourself in someone else's shoes.

Exercise 7.14 What Do These Bears Need?

Can you figure out what these bears really need? Remember, RILEE Bear has all the affection he needs. Draw a line from each of the other bears to the gift of love that will really settle that bear down.

Bear Behaviors	Gifts of Love
1. Intruder Bear	A. approval
2. Blamer Bear	B. attention
3. Circular Bear	C. acknowledgement
4. Wanter Bear	D. attachment
5. Wallower Bear	E. acceptance
6. RILEE Bear	F. affection

Remember, when Intruder Bear feels scared, secure attachment will comfort him. When Blamer Bear feels angry, positive attention will allow him to feel friendly again. When Circular Bear feels anxious, genuine acceptance will calm her down. When Wanter Bear feels embarrassed, lots of approval will make her feel proud. When Wallower Bear feels sad, a good dose of acknowledgment will make him feel glad, and of course, when RILEE Bear gets the affection he needs, he can balance his happy and gloomy feelings.

Answers: 1D, 2B, 3E, 4A, 5C, 6F

Exercise 7.15 What Do These Bears Fear?

Each of the bears in this exercise sometimes feels a very special fear, which we've adapted from Hendrix (1992). Can you figure out what each bear really fears? Loss of control would be RILEE Bear's fear, but since he knows how to control his own behavior, he is not so afraid of other people trying to control him. Draw a line from each of the other bears to the fear that each one needs to resolve.

Bear Behaviors	Developmental Fears
1. Intruder Bear	A. shame
2. Blamer Bear	B. being alone
3. Circular Bear	C. loss
4. Wanter Bear	D. abandonment
5. Wallower Bear	E. failure
6. RILEE Bear	F. loss of control

Again, it is easy for Intruder Bear to believe that he might be abandoned at any moment. At such times, secure attachment will create a sense of comfort for him. When Blamer Bear believes that he is about to be lost forever, friendly attention will soothe him. When Circular Bear believes that people are ashamed of her, calm acceptance is needed. When Wanter Bear believes that she is about to fail, proud approval is needed. When Wallower Bear believes that he will end up all alone, acknowledgment will make him feel glad. But as you know, RILEE Bear has all the affection he needs, so he has learned how to balance his happy and gloomy feelings and to be in control of his behavior. Nobody needs to control RILEE Bear because he has learned to do this himself.

Answers: 1D, 2C, 3A, 4E, 5B, 6F

Exercise 7.16 What Kind of Bear Are You?

Have all family members pick the behavior that you each use the most when you are upset. What kind of bear do you become? Write down the answers to the following questions.

A. Which behavior is it? What kind of bear do you become? Circle one.

    Intruder   Blamer   Circular   Wanter   Wallower

B. What conflict occurs in your family when you choose this behavior?

_____

C. Why do you think this happens?

_____

D. What fears drive this behavior?

_____

E. What needs would resolve this behavior?

_____

Remember, when these troublesome bears come to visit, it's your choice to either let them in or send them away. Don't let them overwhelm you. Do the following connect-the-dots game for fun, and to celebrate what you've learned.

 Connect the Dots

Have you ever held a pinwheel while it is blowing in the wind? It is such a wonderful feeling—all that energy, all that freedom, right in your own hand. When you give up your fears and accept the gifts of love, you can feel just as free as RILEE with his pinwheel. Connect the dots and create your own RILEE Bear.

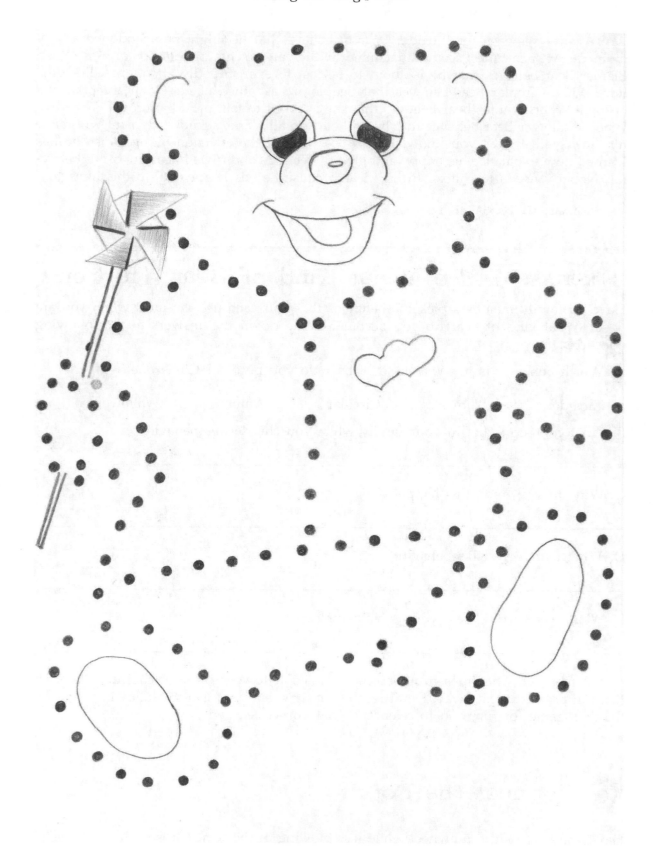

Get Rid of Bothersome Bears

When Intruder Bear, Blamer Bear, Circular Bear, Wanter Bear, and Wallower Bear come to join you, you can get rid of them by changing your feelings.

To get rid of	You must
1. Intruder Bear	decrease scary feelings, increase comfy feelings
2. Blamer Bear	decrease angry feelings, increase friendly feelings
3. Circular Bear	decrease anxious feelings, increase calm feelings
4. Wanter Bear	decrease embarrassed feelings, increase proud feelings
5. Wallower Bear	decrease sad feelings, increase glad feelings

6. You don't want to get rid of RILEE Bear, but this requires flexibility. You must decrease happy feelings when they are just pretend and allow yourself to feel gloomy when and where those feelings are real.

Though you are able to get rid of those other bears, simply changing your feelings does not get rid of Reactor Bear, Challenger Bear, and Teaser Bear. Just changing how you feel is not enough to deal with these very badly behaving bears. You'll learn more about how to get rid of Reactor Bear, Challenger Bear, and Teaser Bear in the next chapter.

Do you know how to change how you feel? *You must recognize what you are saying to yourself and think the opposite thought.* You must give it your best effort. You can do it! I have confidence in you. So let's practice changing your thoughts. Remember to practice your relaxation exercises to help you change your thoughts. Breathing out those angry thoughts can really make it easier to change them. Then your feelings will change. But it requires practice.

Exercise 7.16 Choosing RILEE Thoughts

Here are ten scenarios based on Murphy and Oberlin's ten angry traits (2001). How do you change from the angry path to the RILEE path? Again, please make copies of these pages or use a blank sheet of paper so that every member in your family may participate. Remind yourself to breathe deeply, to relax your muscles, to choose RILEE thoughts, and to say, "I can feel comfy and safe, any time, any place."

1. From misery to joy:

    "It was raining and raining and I had to stay home all day."

    Write down your angry thought and change it to a RILEE thought. Just flip the relationship coin and think the exact opposite thought.

    Miserable thought _____

    _____

    Joyful thought _____

    _____

2. From confusion to clarity:

"Dad said I could watch TV, but I had to watch the Home Improvement Channel with him. I was getting a double bind message from Dad. Do it, but do it my way."

Write down your angry thought and change it to a RILEE thought. Just flip the relationship coin and think the exact opposite thought.

Confusing thought _____

_____

Clear thought _____

_____

3. From blaming to taking responsibility:

"I was blaming my classmate because I failed my math test."

Write down your angry thought and change it to a RILEE thought. Just flip the relationship coin and think the exact opposite thought.

Blaming thought _____

_____

Owning thought _____

_____

4. From feeling mad to feeling good:

"I was feeling bad and getting mad because Mom wouldn't let me go to the ball game."

Write down your angry thought and change it to a RILEE thought. Just flip the relationship coin and think the exact opposite thought.

Mad thought _____

_____

Good thought _____

_____

5. From lacking empathy to having empathy:

"My sister had just been teased by her girlfriends for being overweight."

Write down your angry thought and change it to a RILEE thought. Just flip the relationship coin and think the exact opposite thought.

Unempathic thought _____

_____

Empathic thought _____

_____

6. From being defensive to being positive:

"Mom's bracelet was missing. She had asked me to put it away in her jewelry box, but I didn't do it."

Write down your angry thought and change it to a RILEE thought. Just flip the relationship coin and think the exact opposite thought.

Defensive thought _____

_____

Offensive thought _____

_____

7. From enjoying power to enjoying relatedness:

"Dad will let me decide whether or not my younger brother, with whom I've just had a fight, gets to go with me to the party."

Write down your angry thought and change it to a RILEE thought. Just flip the relationship coin and think the exact opposite thought.

Power thought _____

_____

Relatedness thought _____

_____

8. From destructive to constructive self-talk:

"I missed hitting the last pitch of the baseball game, and our team lost."

Write down your angry thought and change it to a RILEE thought. Just flip the relationship coin and think the exact opposite thought.

Destructive thought _____

_____

Constructive thought _____

_____

9. From anger to balance:

"My cousin is coming over to babysit for me. I don't think I need a babysitter."

Write down your angry thought and change it to a RILEE thought. Just flip the relationship coin and think the exact opposite thought.

Angry thought _____

_____

Balanced thought _____

_____

10. From manipulating to relating:

"I want to wear my sister's letter jacket. I am trying to figure out the best way to get her to let me wear it."

Write down your angry thought and change it to a RILEE thought. Just flip the relationship coin and think the exact opposite thought.

Manipulative thought _____

_____

Kind thought _____

_____

Now, compare your answers with your family's answers. See what choices in thinking each of you made. Remember that breathing out the angry thoughts will help you flip to the RILEE thoughts.

All this work means you're no longer a beginner on the *Karate dō*—RILEE path. Play the following game to continue to practice managing your anger.

 # RILEE Karate Game

Directions: Color some paper strips purple, green, and brown and one strip black to use as belts. Each person rolls a die to determine his or her color. If you roll a one or three, you are to respond like a purple belt. Likewise, if you roll a two or four, you are to respond like a green belt, and if you roll a five, you are to respond like a brown belt. Whoever rolls a six first gets to serve as the black belt master and gets to help the other players. Ten scenarios are included. Each contestant gets to respond to the situation card that's the same as his or her color. This time no one is just a beginner.

Contestants

Purple (1, 3)

Green (2, 4)

Brown (5)

Black/coach (6)

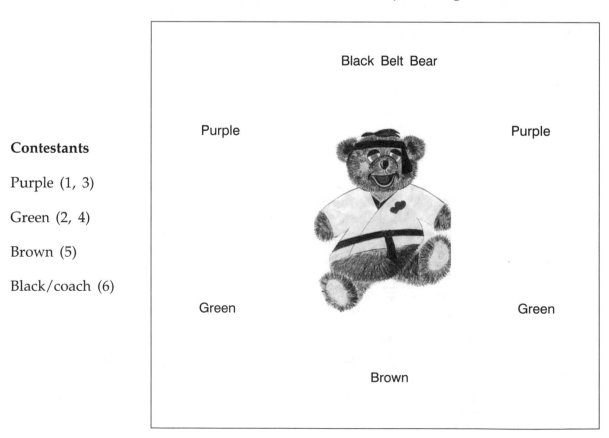

Roll the dice again to determine who will go first. When you choose your card, talk about a similar situation that happened to you. Remember, as you act out your response to the situation on the card, respond according to your color and level of mastery.

RILEE Karate Situation Cards

(color me purple) It was raining, and the party was cancelled.	(color me green) I was getting a double bind message from Mom. She was smiling but telling me to stop clowning around.
(color me purple) I blamed my friend for not getting the lead role in the play.	(color me green) I was feeling mad because Dad took away my toys.
(color me purple) My friend was teased because she has curly hair.	(color me green) Mom's glasses were missing. She had asked me to put them on her desk, but I didn't do it.
(color me brown) Dad will not let me decide whether or not my sister gets to go with me to the movie.	(color me brown) I missed the foul shot that would have won the game.
(color me black) My parents won't let me stay at home by myself, but I don't want to go to the grocery store with them.	(color me black) I want to play with my brother's new game, but he won't let me.

Include the following behaviors in your responses.

Intermediate Behaviors
(purple/green)

* Formal behavior
* Good effort
* Lack of serenity
* Weak character

Advanced Behaviors
(brown)

* Formal behavior
* Best effort
* Lack of serenity
* Strong character

Master Behaviors
(black)

* Formal behavior
* Best effort
* Serenity
* Strong character

Before you begin, there is one more important part to this RILEE Karate Game. You get to kick, punch, and shout! But you must follow these rules.

* If you are a purple or green belt, you can kick or punch, but only if you can do so without anger and without hurting anyone or anything. Remember to breathe deeply, to relax your muscles, to choose RILEE thoughts, and to say, "I can feel comfy and safe, any time, any place."

* An advnced belt (brown) can shout, but only if you can do so without anger and without using bad language. Remember the family contracts you made. No teasing, blaming, excess wanting, or fairness challenging is allowed.

* If you are the black belt master, you display a commanding masterful presence based on the FACTS. You can do or say anything that shows self-mastery.

Congratulations! You are no longer a beginner. You are really a black belt master in the making. Good job. Now let's proceed to chapter 8. There you will learn how to control Reactor, Challenger, and Teaser Bears' bad behaviors. These bears are not real masters, because their behaviors are based on anger. They are always on red alert. Remember, knowledge is real power.

chapter 8

How to Master
Your Anger

Thoughts and body sensations influence your feelings. Feelings influence your actions. But it's the choices you make that determine the outcome. This chapter is about choices. Every time you choose actions that hurt you or hurt others, you are out of control. When you choose actions that help you and help others, you are in control.

Remember the karate principle: *Acting on anger is not okay*. Acting with control is the RILEE way. In chapter 7 your learned how to manage your anger. Now, it's time to learn to control it from beginning to end. Managing anger is about *intervention*. Controlling the thoughts, sensations, feelings, and actions that produce anger is about *prevention*. This chapter is about prevention. *You can choose to be in control*. You can choose to take charge, to be an advanced, skillful person. We are ready to introduce you to some techniques that are clearly on an advanced, brown belt level. You are on your way to mastery.

The First Step: For Parents

Everyone experiences breakdowns in caring along the developmental path. Each of us was raised by other human beings, some of whom did the best they could and some of whom did not.

For you to be an effective parent, you must be a good teacher. In order to be a good teacher, you must have a good understanding of your developmental stages. Breaks in caregiver relationships lead to behavioral hostility (Diamond and Liddle 1999). These breakdowns usually involve trust, commitment, power, love, and protection. Such breakdowns usually lead to histories of neglect, betrayal, abandonment, and abuse. You must understand your wounds so you do not pass those wounds onto your children. You may say, "I would never do that," but often these unresolved wounds are unintentionally repeated. Remember, the most fundamental form of learning is imitation. Thus, you might inadvertently imitate one of these painful breakdowns in caring before you know it. Hopefully, this exercise will put you in charge of your choices. So, let's examine a significant breakdown in caring that you may have experienced. Work hard to remember. There is no advantage to saying, "My childhood was perfect. Nothing like this ever happened to me." Even if you believe that your childhood was perfect, do your best to remember:

Was it an issue of	Did you feel	Did you choose to
trust?	betrayed?	mistrust others?
commitment?	abandoned?	manipulate rather than relate?
power?	neglected?	vie for power?
love?	rejected?	love conditionally?
protection?	abused?	strike first, ask second?

If you have held onto any of these old coping strategies (to mistrust, manipulate, maintain power, manage through conditional love, or strike first), you cannot be an effective parent or teacher. Wynne (1984) concludes that families must have trust and attachment to communicate effectively and solve problems. Support and connectedness make a difference. Conflict and isolation merely breed anger, which Diamond and Liddle (1999) refer to as "behavioral hostility."

The Second Step: For the Family

Changing your behavior can bring joy and peace to you and your family. By remembering your developmental bad days and how they gave birth to your issues, you can make better choices. You can choose to create joy. It is hard to hurt someone who is supportive of you and to whom you are connected in the RILEE way.

When you are out of control, it is easy to

* Slam doors

* Scream and yell

* Say mean things

* Hit, kick, or punch someone

* Break things

When you are in control, it is possible to

* Listen effectively

* Understand the situation

* Be considerate of others

* Problem-solve efficiently

* Express yourself properly

Exercise 8.1 Remember When

Now, go back in time and allow yourself to remember a bad day in your life. Find one from your childhood, look somewhere between the ages of five and fifteen for this event. Write it down here so that you can recognize its place in your development.

"My bad day was _____

_____

_____

_____

_____

_____."

1. Which of the five breakdown issues in caring—trust, commitment, power, love, or protection—did this day include? Write about it below.

"My breakdown issue in caring was _____

_____

_____."

2. Which of the five breakdown feelings did you experience? Did you feel betrayed, abandoned, neglected, rejected, or abused. Write about it below.

"My breakdown feeling was _____

_____

_____."

3. Allow yourself to know which of the five unwise coping strategies you adopted. Did you learn this and other similar experiences to mistrust others, manipulate rather than relate, vie for power, love unconditionally, or strike first, ask second? Write about it below.

"The bad day coping strategy I chose was _____

_____

_____."

Being out of control is a choice. Being in control is a choice. Remember, evaluation is about your behavior, not about you as a person. Therefore, *choosing* in control behaviors is good. Choosing out of control behaviors is bad. Again, it is about your choices, not about you as a person. Exhibiting mastery is about being in control of your behavior. Being in control of your behavior is about making wise *choices*. Wise choices come from

1. Listening. You can't talk and listen at the same time.

2. Understanding. You must pay attention to what is being said.

3. Considering. You must consider how people feel, you included.

4. Problem-solving. You must think about several different options.

5. Communicating. You must talk these options over with others before choosing one.

When you use this five step process and when you are supportively connected to the important people in your life, you will be able to prevent your anger from becoming your master. This is very important. You must be the master of your anger. Your anger must not master you.

Why Do You Need to Control Your Anger?

It isn't fun being angry. Being angry can make you feel pretty bad inside. When you aren't in control of your anger, it can get you into a lot of trouble. It isn't fun being around people who are always angry, especially when they aren't in control of their anger. Think about how things would be if everyone (your parents, teachers, and friends) went around screaming, yelling, or hitting things when they got angry. You wouldn't like to be around them very much, right? Try to remember that other people feel the same way about you. It is much easier to make friends when you are in control of your anger, when you are a brown belt.

What happens when you are in control of your anger?

Exercise 8.2 Remember When You Lost Control

It may seem like you are in control when you slam doors or yell and scream or break things, but really you're not. Think about the last time you were out of control of your anger. Then answer these questions.

1. When was the last time you were out of control of your anger? _____

_____

_____

2. What did you think? _____

_____

_____

3. What did you feel? _____

_____

_____

4. What did you sense? _____

_____

_____

5. What actions did you choose? _____

_____

_____

6. What was the outcome? _____

_____

_____

Usually the outcome involves hurting others, and that's not okay. In the long run, you hurt yourself. Choose wisely, avoid pain.

Take charge of your anger. Be the master! It is easier to do this when you know that expressing anger is a choice. The following story is an example of how anger is a choice.

Tommy's Story

Tommy just joined the baseball team. He was not very good at catching the ball, and some of the boys on the team began teasing him. Tommy did not like being teased by those boys. He could have gotten mad and started a fight with them, but instead he told himself, "I'm just learning how to play baseball. I'm trying my best, and the coach says I'm doing a good job, so I just won't listen to what those boys are saying." Tommy made the choice not to be angry.

Before You Get Angry—STOP!

When something happens that you do not like, it is up to you to decide if you are going to get angry or not. Ask yourself: Is this something really worth getting mad about, or should I just keep my cool and not let this get to me. You can choose not to express anger.

Remember, though, that everyone gets angry sometimes. Feeling angry is okay. Acting on anger is not okay, especially if you damage property or hurt yourself or someone else. The point is to not act on your anger. When you do this, you will be a brown belt master.

So, *think before you act*. Ask yourself, "Okay, I'm angry. Now what am I going to do about it?" Think about what would happen if you let your anger get out of control.

Think about it: Remember the story of Tommy on the baseball team? What do you think would have happened if he had started a fight with those boys who were teasing him? Do you think he made a good choice not to allow his anger to control him, but to be a brown belt master instead?

Exercise 8.3 Are These Wise (FACTS) or Painful (FATs) Choices?

Read the following stories and decide if the people in the stories are in control of their anger.

1. Jane went to the movies with her friend, Beth. Jane and Beth were sharing a box of popcorn. During the movie, Beth spilled the box of popcorn all over the floor. Jane was very angry because she had bought the popcorn. Jane started yelling at Beth, "Beth, you are so clumsy! I should have never agreed to share my popcorn with you. Go and buy me another box right now, or I'm not going to speak to you anymore!"

   Is Jane in control of her anger? Explain your answer. _____

   _____

   _____

   _____

   _____

2. Ricardo was supposed to meet his brother, Lucas, at the library at 4:00 P.M. They were going to go to a volleyball game. Lucas had been waiting for almost thirty minutes. He was getting angry because the game had already started. When Ricardo finally arrived, Lucas said, "Ricardo, you were supposed to be here at 4:00 P.M. I've been waiting here for a long time. Why are you so late?" Ricardo explained that he had to stay after school and finish an assignment for his teacher. "Well, that's okay," Lucas said. "I bet we haven't missed much of the game. Let's go."

   Is Lucas in control of his anger? Explain your answer. _____

   _____

   _____

   _____

   _____

3. Kendra asked her friend, Vanessa, to go to the mall with her on Saturday. Vanessa said she could go, but on Friday night Vanessa called Kendra to tell her she was not feeling well and that she would have to stay home on Saturday. The next morning, Kendra and her mother went to the mall. They were just leaving the pet store when Kendra saw Vanessa there with her new friend, Gina. Kendra was so mad! She thought, "How could Vanessa do this to me?" Kendra decided to wait until she had calmed down to talk to Vanessa.

Is Kendra in control of her anger? Explain your answer. _____

_____

_____

_____

_____

4. Michael really wanted a new baseball glove. His mother told him that she would buy him one if he helped mow the grass and clean up the garage. A few days later, Michael and his mother went to the sports store. Michael asked if he could have the baseball glove since he was going to mow the grass and clean the garage on Saturday. His mother said, "No, Michael. We made a deal. You can have the glove after you've helped with the lawn and the garage." Michael got angry. He started yelling at his mother, "You never let me do anything! I told you I would do my chores. It's just not fair!" When Michael got home, he ran to his room and slammed the door.

Is Michael in control of his anger? Explain your answer. _____

_____

_____

_____

_____

Exercise 8.4 You Choose

Now that you understand the difference between wise (FACTS) and painful (FATs) choices, let's see how well you would do in the following. Write down what you would do to be in control instead of letting your anger be in control. Be sure to choose a behavior that would not hurt you or anyone else.

1. You've been planning to go to your friend's house all day long. Right before you are ready to leave, your mom tells you that you cannot go because you did not clean up your room. At first you got really mad. But, instead of fighting with your mom, you could _____

_____

_____

2. Your older brother is always teasing you because you are shorter than he is. He really makes you angry, because you do not like to be teased. Instead of trying to get back at him, you could _____

_____

_____

3. You ask your teacher for a bathroom pass, and she tells you that you cannot have one because recess is in five minutes. You do not like to be told no. Instead of "smarting off" to your teacher, you could _____

_____

_____

It's important to remember to relax. Practice relaxing with the following relaxation exercise.

Exercise 8.5 RILEE Relaxation

Directions: Parents, read the following exercise aloud while your children lie comfortably with room to move. Let them act out what the exercise tells them.

Here I am
Back again
I'm Rilee, the
Re-lax-a-tion Bear
Here to remind you
of all you learned in
earlier exercises

So—wrinkle your nose
Wiggle your toes
Put a big smile on your lips and
A twinkle in your eye
and say,
"I can be comfy and safe,
Any time, any place."

So let's do it right now.
Take a deep, deep, deep breath,
Tighten all, all, all of your muscles
From your face, face, face
to your toes, toes, toes
tight, tight, tight
Now, hold, hold, hold
Now, loose, loose, loose
Let your breath go, go, go
But slow, slow, slow
and say,
"I can be comfy and safe,

Any time, any place."
Good job.
You have just relaxed the RILEE way.

Now, lie down
with your back on the ground,
Wrinkle your nose,
Wiggle your toes,
Put a big smile on your lips
And a twinkle in your eye
and say,
"I can be comfy and safe,
any time, any place."

So let's do it again
Take a deep, deep, deep breath
Tighten all, all, all of your muscles
From your face, face, face
to your toes, toes, toes
tight, tight, tight
Now, hold, hold, hold
Now, loose, loose, loose
Let your breath go, go, go
But slow, slow, slow,
and say,
"I can be comfy and safe,
Any time, any place."

When you think calm, comfy thoughts
And feel cool, safe feelings,
When you tighten and loosen all of your
muscles,
When you breathe in deeply
And breathe out slowly,
You are relaxing the RILEE way.

Let's add another dimension,
A new way to create and
relieve all that tension.
Pretend you have two squeeze balls,
One in each hand,
Now raise your arms
high, high, high
In the air, air, air.
Squeeze the balls
tight, tight, tight
Hold, hold, hold.
Let your arms
down, down, down
Slow, slow, slow.
Let your fists
go, go, go.
Good job.

Now raise your legs
high, high, high
In the air, air, air.
Spread your toes
out, out, out,
Hold, hold, hold.
Let your legs
down, down, down
Slow, slow, slow.
Let your toes
go, go, go.
Good job.

Now, open your jaw
wide, wide, wide.
Take a deep, deep breath.
Put your tongue down, down, down
Hold, hold, hold that breath
So you will
yawn, yawn, yawn
As you breathe out slow, slow, slow.
Put your first finger in your
mouth, mouth, mouth and
Close, close, close
That's right. Close.
Until your lips are just a finger
apart, apart, apart
That's right.

Now remove your finger and leave your lips
A little apart, part, part
Good job.
You have just relaxed the RILEE way.

Remember, when you are
very, very, very tense and want to relax
Quick, quick, quick
Just make yourself
yawn, yawn, yawn
Then put your finger in your
mouth, mouth, mouth
Close, close, close
Slow, slow, slow
Until your lips are just a little
Apart, part, part
And let all your jaw tension
go, go, go.

Remember, whenever you need to relax
quick, quick, quick
Yawn, yawn, yawn
Slow, slow, slow and
Allow your lips to remain
a little apart, part, part
and all your jaw tension will
go, go, go.

Good job!
You are really catching on to the
RILEE relaxation way.

So, when you want to relax,
remember to say,
"I can feel comfy and safe,
any time, any place."

Remember to breathe deeply
In and out
Remember to tighten and
loosen all of your muscles
up and down
remember to think calm, comfy thoughts
remember to feel cool, safe feelings
and you will be relaxing the RILEE way.

Now, for a time
when you are very, very, very
scared or angry
and you need to be calm and comfy
Quick, quick, quick
You can raise your arms
High, high, high
And squeeze your hands
Tight, tight, tight
Or you can raise your legs
Up, up, up
And stretch you toes

Out, out, out
Or you can drop your jaw
Down, down, down
Or you can do all three, three, three
And breathe in and out
In, in, in
Out, out, out
Up, up, up
Down, down, down
Arms, legs, jaw

Tight, tight, tight
Loose, loose, loose
And you will relax
Quick, quick, quick
You will feel comfy and safe
The RILEE way, way, way.

Congratulations! You are learning to relax
fast, fast, fast by mastering
one, two, or all three
of the RILEE ways.

The Third Step: Brown Belt Mastery

It's time for the family to confront Reactor Bear, Challenger Bear, and Teaser Bear. These bears are always on red alert. They are always angry. They are always looking for someone to dump on. RILEE Bear can tell you that when you display brown belt mastery, these badly behaving bears will sense your inner peace, and they will move on. When you do not play victim, they will move on. These nasty cousins enjoy getting to you. They enjoy seeing you in pain. They enjoy breaking your spirit. When you choose to remain in control of your actions, when you keep your thoughts positive, when you feel good about yourself, these nasty bears do not have a chance. They can inflict pain on you only if you let them. When they come a-knocking on your FATS door, choose not to let them in. Here's how.

Teaser Bear

When Teaser Bear comes to call, remind yourself that there will always be a little bit of truth in what he says. *So, acknowledge what is true.* Next, remind yourself that he will try to shame you by revealing what you are trying to keep a secret. *So, refuse to keep secrets*—yours or others'. He will then try to agitate you to make you cry. *So, remember to keep yourself calm.* He will also try to tease you in front of others so that you will not be able to protect yourself. *So, ask those around you for help.* If all else fails, Teaser Bear will try to get you to lose control. *So, stay calm and walk away.*

It takes a brown belt master to walk away. Anyone can lose control. Only a brown belt master can remain in control when Teaser Bear comes calling. Remember, remaining in control is an internal process, not an external display! If you have to show how powerful you are (for that is what Teaser Bear encourages), then you are not really powerful at all. Be powerful. Be in control of yourself.

Challenger Bear

When Challenger Bear comes to visit, remind yourself that you will not be able to maintain the expert position. He will challenge all the statements you make, regardless of whether they are statements of fact or statements of feeling. *So, be reflective rather than authoritative.* Since Challenger Bear loves to argue, *be related rather than combative.* Since Challenger Bear loves to win, *make winning easy for him.* Since Challenger Bear loves to fight, *be passive rather than active in your responses.* And since Challenger Bear loves to make you feel inferior, *maintain eye contact. Do not look down or away.*

Reactor Bear

When Reactor Bear comes to visit, remember that this is the way she gets attention, *so give her positive attention before she reacts.* Remember that she usually is not heard because of all her antics, *so listen to what she is saying.* Since she is usually not acknowledged for having good ideas, *acknowledge her positive ideas.* Since she is not a good problem-solver, *help her to find new ways of looking at the situation.* But most important, since she is usually inconsistent in her behaviors, *be consistent in your responses.*

Whether you are dealing with a teaser bear, challenger bear, or reactor bear, preventing yourself from becoming angry is the key to responding. Remember, someone will always be there to take you on. It is your job to display brown belt mastery by not allowing yourself to be manipulated by the unwise choices of others. Those who tease, challenge, and/or overreact are making unwise choices. They are creating pain for themselves and others. Do not join them in this process. Maintain brown belt mastery instead.

To master Teaser Bear, recognize and reveal his angry *actions.* Don't allow yourself to become a victim of his angry actions. Make FACTS choices:

1. Be truthful

2. Have no secrets

3. Be calm

4. Get help

5. Walk away

To master Challenger Bear, recognize and reveal his angry *thoughts.* Don't allow yourself to fight with his angry thoughts. Make FACTS choices:

1. Reflect

2. Relate

3. Be passive

4. Concede

5. Make eye contact

To master Reactor Bear, recognize and reveal her angry *feelings.* Don't allow yourself to be overwhelmed by her angry feelings. Make FACTS choices:

1. Attend

2. Listen

3. Acknowledge

4. Help

5. Be consistent

From Red Alert to Brown Alert

When you make FACTS choices, your body will be able to change from red alert to brown alert. Here is the brown alert formula for brown belt mastery:

1. sensing a problem

2. keeping yourself comfy and calm any time, any place

3. recognizing and revealing others' angry thoughts

4. making wise FACTS choices.

For brown belt mastery practice, play the RILEE Karate Game once again. This time, you can choose advanced behaviors. Show off your new skills. You can do it!

 # RILEE Karate Game

Directions: Color five paper strips brown and one strip black to use as belts. Roll a die to determine your color. If you roll a one, two, three, four, or five, you're a brown belt. If you roll a six, you're the black belt master. Twelve scenarios are included. Each brown belt gets to respond to a situation card using advanced brown belt mastery behaviors. The black belt master responds to his or her situation card and is available to help others.

Contestants

Brown (1–5)

Black (6)

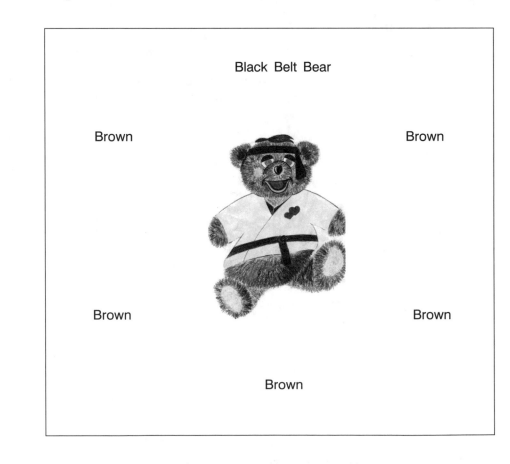

When everyone's ready, roll the die again to see who will go first. Remember, when you choose your card, talk about a similar situation that happened to you. As you act out your response to the situation on the card, remember to behave like a brown belt. Or, like a black belt if you are the black belt master.

RILEE Karate Situation Cards

(color me brown) Someone calls you stupid.	(color me brown) Your brother tries to hit you.
(color me brown) Your sister is talking nonstop.	(color me brown) Your mom is really, really upset.
(color me brown) Someone is gossiping about your best friend.	(color me brown) Your sister wants you to keep a secret.
(color me brown) A bully is in your face.	(color me brown) Your friend tells you that you don't know what you are talking about.
(color me brown) Your cousin has several ideas, all of which will lead to trouble.	(color me brown) Your sister can't make up her mind about what to wear to a party, and keeps asking you, while you're waiting to leave.
(color me black) A bully is trying to agitate you.	(color me black) Someone is inviting you to behave impulsively.

Include the following behaviors in your responses.

Advanced Behaviors (brown)	**Mastery Behaviors** (black)
Formal behavior	Formal behavior
Best effort	Best effort
Lack of serenity	Serenity
Strong character/experienced decision making	Strong character/strong decision making

Again, this is karate, so you can kick, punch, and shout! But you must follow these rules.

* If you are a brown belt, you can kick, punch, and shout, but only if you can do so without anger and without contact—only if you can show an advanced brown belt presence. Contact means no touching, breaking, or striking.

* If you are the black belt master, you should display a commanding masterful presence based on the FACTS. You can do or say anything that shows black belt mastery, or you can guide others in their efforts at advanced brown belt behavior.

Congratulations! You now know how to respond rather than react. You know how to choose wise behaviors. You can now control your FATs for you have mastered the C and made FATs into FACTS. Good job! Now it's time to proceed to chapter 9 where you will learn to Be Heard, Not Hurt. You can do it. You can and will achieve your black belt of mastery.

PART III

Good Relating: The Next Four Steps

Are you prepared to be a related parent? Do you think that parenting is about power and control? Or do you realize that good parenting is about personal mastery? Do you understand that good parenting is about keeping yourself calm even in the most chaotic situation? Do you know that good parenting is about being a good facilitator? Are you aware that good parenting is about being heard, not about being angry?

In Part III, we will talk about how good parenting is about relating, not dominating. Specifically, we will show you how to create a relaxed family environment where polite and courteous behaviors prevail. You will learn to speak in a wise voice. You will become an effective listener and communicator. You will come to understand your children's needs and concerns. And you will find ways to help them make good choices. For these are the RILEE tasks of healthy family life.

chapter 9

Be Heard,
Not Hurt

Anger can serve different roles in different families. According to Murphy and Oberlin (2001), anger can serve four different roles in a family: stress, power, pain, and desire. In keeping with our RILEE theory, we have added two more roles: sadness and embarrassment.

Perhaps you've never thought of the role that anger serves in your family. Anger can create considerable *stress* and tension in a family. It is an effective way to cover fears of abandonment or concerns about secure attachment. These fears and needs can be camouflaged by anger. Anger can divert attention away from these more tender issues.

Anger can be a very *powerful* force in a family. It is an effective way to cover a fear of loss and a sense of powerlessness. It forces everyone to focus attention away from the true issues. It is another efficient way to camouflage family problems.

Anger can create considerable *pain* in a family. It is an effective way to divert fears of shame and unfulfilled needs for acceptance. Instead of dealing with these very tender issues, a family can create pain.

Anger can cause considerable *embarrassment* in a family. It is a very loud and effective way to cover fears of failure and disapproval. It forces everyone to feel embarrassed and to retreat into silence. It is a very efficient way to stop family members from stating their needs.

Anger can make family members very *sad*. It is an effective way to maintain feelings of loneliness. When family members are very angry with one another, they feel very much alone. There is no acknowledgement. There is no connection. Even concerns for one another are thwarted by anger. All that prevails is sadness.

Anger can also encourage excessive *desire* in a family. Encouraging a family member's every wish is an effective way to control that person. It creates more and more desire. No one is ever satisfied. This gentle way of controlling others is usually a reaction to the fear of being controlled. It is motivated by anger.

The following table will help you to see how these roles relate to the other concepts, including Hendrix theory (1992) that we've previously discussed. In order to change these angry family roles, new behaviors are required. We suggest the RILEE-dō behaviors listed in the fourth column.

Hendrix Imago Developmental Stages	Hendrix Primary Fears	RILEE Theory of Needs	RILEE-Dō Behaviors	Roles of Family Anger
attachment	abandonment	attachment security	relax	stress
exploration	loss	attention	relate	power
identity	shame	acceptance	forgive	pain
competence	failure	approval	share	embarrassment
concern	being alone	acknowledgement	connect	sadness
intimacy	loss of control	affection	satiate	desire

Several important dynamics occur at each developmental stage. If they are not properly addressed, they become family affective themes (and can return to haunt you at any given moment). But *knowledge*, not anger, is the true power to effect change. By understanding these dynamics and their related FATs, you can choose wiser behaviors. When stressed, you may recall a FATs fear of abandonment. *Relax.* Allow yourself to feel secure. When vying for power, you may recall a FATs fear of loss. *Relate.* Allow yourself to give and receive some attention. When experiencing pain, you may recall a FATs fear of shame. *Forgive.* Accept what is and has been. Remember, forgiveness is about freeing yourself. When feeling embarrassed, you may recall a failure experience. *Share.* Don't keep it a secret. Let others give you their approval for your humanness. When feeling sad, you may remember a time when you were all alone. *Connect.* Let yourself receive warm embraces from those who love you. When you desire something more, you might remember a time when you felt very restricted and controlled by your family. *Satiate.* Allow yourself to feel your family's affection rather than your loved one's limits.

How Anger Functions

In order to do so, however, you must take time to understand the functions anger serves in your family. So, let us review Murphy and Oberlin's four problematic family styles, along with the two that we added (i.e., numbers four and five). They are listed below:

1. "In the frantic family, anger is the voice of stress." (2001, 81)

2. "In the angry family, anger is the voice of power." (2001, 81)

3. "In the troubled family, anger is the voice of pain." (2001, 81)

4. In the defective family, anger is the voice of embarrassment.

5. In the lonely family, anger is the voice of sadness.

6. "In the indulgent family, anger is the voice of desire." (2001, 81)

According to Murphy and Oberlin, frantic families are overscheduled, overwhelmed, and overstressed. Distress, rather than comfort, prevails. Angry families are composed of "angry, short-tempered, critical people" (81). Emotional outbursts rather than rules prevail. Troubled families are often dealing with issues of grief, addiction, mental illness, and/or marital discord. Anxiety and pain, rather than calm acceptance, prevail. Defective families are filled with secrets. Embarrassment, rather than openness, prevails. Lonely families are isolated; cut off from both the outside world and each other. Sadness, rather than connectedness, prevails. Indulgent families are permissive, confused, and conciliatory. Desire and happiness, rather than affection and empathic understanding, prevail.

The Voice of Discipline

In each of these six families, anger serves as an important *voice*. That is why this chapter is about being heard, not hurt. Whether anger is the voice of stress, power, pain, embarrassment, sadness, or desire in your family, using anger to get your way leads only to more problems. You must make wiser choices. It is time to accept the RILEE Karate-dō principle: Acting on anger is not okay.

Acting with control is the RILEE way. This requires being able to *relax* rather than remaining tense. This requires being able to *relate* rather than being controlling. This requires being able to *forgive* rather than holding grudges. This requires being able to *share* rather than keeping secrets. This requires being able to *connect* rather than remaining isolated. This requires being able to *satiate* rather than continuing to be indulgent. All require discipline. It is not easy to make wise choices. It takes a lot of discipline to relax, relate, forgive, share, connect, and satiate. But that is what healthy families do. And so can you. Here's how:

Karate-dō Behaviors → The RILEE Process

1. Relax   →   Practice being comfortable and relaxed together.

2. Relate   →   Do things with one another.

3. Forgive   →   Build a vocabulary of healing, affirming statements.

4. Share   →   Talk to each other every day.

5. Connect   →   Touch each other every day.

6. Satiate   →   Be satisfied with one another.

Find these RILEE Karate-dō matches, in the following exercise.

Exercise 9.1 Matching Examples

Read the statements on the right and see if you can recognize which Karate-dō behaviors they exemplify.

Karate-Dō Behavior

1. relax

2. relate

3 forgive

4. share

5. connect

6. satiate

RILEE Process Statement

____ "I can help you."

____ "I am willing to listen."

____ "I am sorry."

____ "I can feel comfy and safe any time, any place."

____ "I accept your apology."

____ "I can tense and relax my muscles."

____ "I am good enough."

____ "I am pleased with your efforts."

____ "I would like to talk about this."

____ "I feel so relaxed when I am with you."

____ "I would like to give you a hug."

____ "I like when you smile at me."

____ "I would like to give you a kiss."

____ "I like when you consider my point of view."

____ "I like when you value me."

____ "I like when we spend time together."

____ "I like when we go places together."

Answers from top to bottom:
2, 4, 3, 1, 3, 1, 6, 6, 4, 1, 5, 5, 5, 4, 6, 2, 2, 6

Come up with your own RILEE process statements. Use them frequently. Love grows and grows the more it is shared. Relating in love every evening is a wonderful way to live.

The Voice of Anger

Not everybody relates the RILEE Way. Many families relate the angry way. As Murphy and Oberlin (2001) indicated, anger has many voices in families. Anger can be used to share stress, vie for power, experience pain, conceal embarrassment, express sadness, or to show dissatisfaction. No matter what the intent, anger is first and foremost a *voice*.

Think about Hendrix's developmental fears. We will relabel them your FATs fears. Now think about the angry process that you use to maintain those fears. Take a look at the information listed below. Which angry process is most familiar to you? Which one do you use the most? Does it have anything to do with the FATs fears on the left? If your answer was "no" to the last question, look again. See if you can connect the two. Remember, if you know it, you can understand it. If you understand it, you can be free of it. If you are free of it, you can relate the RILEE Way.

FATs Fears	Angry Process
1. Abandonment	Create as much tension as possible.
2. Loss	Control others for power.
3. Shame	Say mean, hurtful things.
4. Failure	Yell at each other.
5. Alone	Slap, kick, and/or punch each other.
6. Control	Be critical and dissatisfied with one another.

Do the next set of exercises with your family.

Exercise 9.2 Match the Fear with the Angry Statement

The angry statements on the left represent unresolved developmental fears, adapted from Hendrix (1992). See if you can recognize which fears these statements help maintain. Be sure to look at the previous table to remind you of the angry process. Then, draw a line from the angry process statement to the fear it rekindles.

FATs Fears	Angry Process Statements
1. abandonment	A. "You need to shut up."
2. loss	B. "You deserved that slap."
3. shame	C. "You can't ever get anything right."
4. failure	D. "You can't go with me."
5. being alone	E. "You deserve to be miserable."
6. loss of control	F. "You are grounded because I said so."

Answers: 1D, 2F, 3C, 4A, 5B, 6E

The "You" Voice

Think about how you use your voice to express anger. More than likely, you use the "you" voice to do so. Statements that begin with "you" are often used to place blame or put someone else down. Using the "you" voice does not allow you to take responsibility for your own actions. Remember RILEE Bear's misbehaving cousins? Teaser Bear, Blamer Bear, Wanter Bear, Challenger Bear, Wallower Bear, Intruder Bear, and Circular Bear regularly use the "you" voice.

Look at these not-so-wise examples of how they speak. Talking this way, these bears never seem to be heard.

Teaser Bear: You look so funny in that dress.

Blamer Bear: You made me late for class.

Wanter Bear: You always get the best piece of cake.

Challenger Bear: You are so wrong.

Wallower Bear: You see, it happened again. Just like last time.

Intruder Bear: You should take me when you go to the movies with your friends.

Circular Bear: You need to let me do it. I know how to figure it out. Let's see:
2 + 2 = 5. I'm sure that's right.

See what a mess the "you" voice can make? RILEE Bear's seven cousins are very good at the "you" voice. They somehow manage to put the responsibility for the problem on someone else's shoulders. That is how they make such a mess of things. When you put the responsibility for your problems on someone else in your family, you can mess things up as well. You can create a lot of pain. You can create a lot of sadness. You can create a lot of turmoil. Is that really what you want? You can live the angry way or the RILEE way. It is your choice.

Three Ways to Behave

There are three ways to behave—the wise way, the wild way, and the weak way.

1. The Wise Way. You stand up for yourself by making your thoughts, feelings, and preferences known in a firm way without hurting yourself or others. You *compromise*.

2. The Wild Way. You stand up for yourself by hurting, threatening, or screaming at others in order to get your way. You *victimize*.

3. The Weak Way. You do not stand up for yourself at all. You allow yourself to become a wimp or a victim. You let others control you. You *pacify*.

Here are three examples:

Weak Wanda

Weak Wanda loaned her favorite pencil to Intruder Irene. Intruder Irene said she would give it back after class. After waiting a couple of days, Weak Wanda whispered to Intruder Irene that she needed her pencil back. Intruder Irene said, "Well, that's too bad because I lost it." Weak Wanda whispered, "Oh, okay," and walked away.

Weak Wanda didn't get her pencil back. She used a *weak, whiny voice*. She should have spoken up and asked for her pencil right after class. If Intruder Irene refused to give it to her, Weak Wanda should have asked the teacher for help.

Wild Willie

Wild Willie was very mad when he found out that Circular Cindy said some bad things about him. Wild Willie ran up to his teacher and started screaming at the top of his lungs that Circular Cindy called him a bad name and that he was going to beat her up. Because he was screaming so loudly, Wild Willie was put in time-out.

Wild Willie did not get any help from his teacher, because he started screaming and was out of control. He was put in time-out because he used a *wild, loud voice*. He ended up hurting himself rather than stopping Circular Cindy from saying bad things about him. Wild Willie should have talked calmly to Circular Cindy about how her words hurt his feelings and made him angry, rather than screaming at his teacher about the problem he was having with Circular Cindy.

Wise RILEE

Wise RILEE let his little brother, Blamer Bob, borrow his new bike to go to his friend Frank's house. Three hours later, Blamer Bob came home, but he had left Wise RILEE's bike at Frank's house. He started to walk away. Wise RILEE looked Blamer Bob in the eye and said in a wise, firm voice: "I let you ride my new bike to Frank's house. I feel angry that you left it there. Go back to Frank's house and bring the bike back with you." Blamer Bob knew that wise RILEE meant business, so he walked back to Frank's house to get the bike.

Wise RILEE got what he wanted because he spoke in a way that made his brother listen to him. He used a *wise, firm voice*. The next time you get angry, you should use the wise, firm voice, too!

Exercise 9.3 Identifying Three Voices

Now, here are three situations. Read each one and circle which voice Shaquille, Elaine, and Shannon used.

1. Shaquille and his sister, Rebecca, were going to the store with their father. It was Shaquille's turn to ride in the front seat of the car, but Rebecca had already gotten into the front seat and wouldn't move. Shaquille said, "Rebecca, I know you want to ride in the front, but we made an agreement to take turns riding in the front seat. Please move to the back, so I can get in. You can ride in the front on the way home."

   Shaquille was using the _____ voice.

   wild   wise   weak

2. Elaine's mother had promised to take her to the park on Saturday if she finished all her homework every night during the week. Elaine worked hard all week, finishing her assignment each night. On Saturday, Elaine was getting ready to go to the park, when her mother told her that they wouldn't be going anywhere because she was too tired and it was too hot outside. Even though Elaine was angry with her mother for breaking her promise, she didn't say anything to her. Elaine went up to her room and cried.

   Elaine was using the _____ voice.

   wild   wise   weak

3. Shannon asked his mother if he could go to his friend's house to play. His mother said he couldn't go because she needed him to stay home and watch his little sister. Shannon yelled, "Mom, you're so mean! You never let me do anything! I don't want to stay home and watch my stupid little sister!"

   Shannon was using the _____ voice.

   wild   wise   weak

Exercise 9.4 Using Each Voice

Read each of the following situations and answer the questions.

You are standing in line at the theater and someone breaks in line and gets in front of you.

1. What could you say or do that would be "weak"? _____

   _____

2. What could you say or do that would be "wild"?_____

   _____

3. What could you say or do that would be "wise"? _____

_____

    Your sister promised to give you $5 for washing her car. You washed her car last week, and she still hasn't paid you.

1. What could you say or do that would be "weak"? _____

_____

2. What could you say or do that would be "wild"? _____

_____

3. What could you say or do that would be "wise"? _____

_____

Exercise 9.5 Were You Heard?

Think of the last time you remember behaving like one of RILEE Bear's nasty cousins. Did you use a weak voice or a wild voice? Were you heard? What was the outcome? Give an example in each case below. Circle whether you used a weak or a wild voice, and describe the outcome.

Teaser Bear weak/wild

    Example_____

_____

    Outcome _____

_____

Blamer Bear weak/wild

    Example_____

_____

    Outcome _____

_____

Wanter Bear weak/wild

    Example_____

_____

Outcome _____

_____

Challenger Bear weak/wild

    Example_____

    _____

    Outcome _____

    _____

Wallower Bear weak/wild

    Example_____

    _____

    Outcome _____

    _____

Intruder Bear weak/wild

    Example_____

    _____

    Outcome _____

    _____

Circular Bear weak/wild

    Example_____

    _____

    Outcome _____

    _____

When you behave like any of these seven bears, your voice is hurtful to others. Most likely, you weren't heard either. Probably, you were hurt yourself. Yes, when you behave like any one of RILEE Bear's nasty cousins (whether you use a weak or a wild voice), you will be hurt, not heard. This is not a good idea. So, you may wish to choose another way to be heard. The "I" voice can be a better approach, if you use it wisely. Here's how.

The "I" Voice

The "I" voice can be either weak, wild, or wonderfully wise. It all depends on how you use it. You can choose your tone of voice each and every time you speak. You can choose your words and phrases. You can choose your inflections. This is not an automatic process, it is a choice you make. When you choose wisely, you can be wonderfully effective.

Just as weak and wild "you" voices do not work, neither do weak and wild "I" voices. But wonderfully wise "I" voices do work. They allow you to *be heard, not hurt*. You can do it. But remember, "I" voices require being relaxed, related, forgiving, sharing, connected, and satiated. They require the RILEE Karate-dō discipline of a black belt master.

Exercise 9.6 Practice Using the Weak, Wild, and Wise Voices

Let's see you practice this mastery in your family. Go back to exercise 9.1 and have each family member take turns reading a RILEE statement three times. First, use a weak voice. Second, use a wild voice. Third, use a wonderfully wise voice. Talk about it. Which one worked? Why did it work?

Which wise voice did you like best? Remember this wise voice and put it in your luggage to use again and again. You can be heard, not hurt, just like RILEE Bear. But remember to keep yourself calm and comfy inside. Just in case you have forgotten, RILEE Bear has returned to help you relax one more time. Remember, another way to prepare to be heard, not hurt, is to use relaxation exercises.

Exercise 9.7 RILEE Relaxation

Directions: Parents, read the following exercise aloud while your children lie comfortably with room to move. Let them act out what the exercise tells them.

Here I am
Back again.
I'm RILEE, the
Re-lax-a-tion Bear
Here to remind you
Of all you learned
In the other exercises
so that you can
Be Heard, Not Hurt.

You can do it.
You can choose wisely.
You can choose a
Strong, strong, strong
voice.
You can choose a
clear, clear, clear
message.
You can choose a
Firm, firm, firm
tone.
You can choose to
be heard, heard, heard,
But respectfully.

So, wrinkle your nose,
Wiggle your toes,
Put a smile on you lips
and a twinkle in your eye.
Drop your jaw, relax,
and say,

"I can be comfy and safe,
any time, any place."

Good. You can do it!
Remember to use
The "I" voice
when you wish to
Be heard.
Remember to take a
deep, deep, deep breath.

Remember to
Relax, relax, relax.
The RILEE

Way, way, way.
Remember to tighten
All, all, all of your muscles
From your face, face, face
down to your
Toes, toes, toes.
Now breathe, breathe, breathe,
Tighten, tighten, tighten,
Hold, hold, hold.
Now, loosen, loosen, loosen.
Let your breath go, go, go.
Good, good, good.

Now say to yourself,
"I can feel comfy and safe,
any time, any place."

Yes, you can.
You can feel comfy and safe,
any time, any place.
For when you breathe deeply
and relax all of your muscles,
when you say
"I can feel comfy and safe,
any time any place,"
you will be ready to
Be Heard, Not Hurt.

You can do it
You can make wise RILEE choices.
You can be a black belt master,
just like me.

So wrinkle your nose,
Wiggle your toes,
Put a smile on your lips,
and a twinkle in your eye.

Drop your jaw
and be a RILEE relaxation
black belt master, just like me.

Now you are truly prepared to
Be Heard, not Hurt.
Congratulations!

Putting it All Together

When you are relaxed, when you use the "I" voice, and when you use the "wonderfully wise" way of speaking, you will be heard, not hurt. But this takes practice.

When something is really important to you, leave Teaser Bear, Blamer Bear, Wanter Bear, Challenger Bear, Wallower Bear, Intruder Bear, and Circular Bear on the shelf amidst your other stuffed toys. Remember, these bears are so full of themselves that they cannot possibly help you be heard, not hurt. If you should bring them along, more than likely, you will be hurt, not heard. Instead, choose wisely.

First, *relax*. Remember to say, "I can feel comfy and safe, any time any place."

Second, *relate*. Remember to say, "I appreciate your time."

Third, *forgive*. Remember to say, "I'm sorry," or, "I forgive you."

Fourth, *share*. Remember to say, "I really love you."

Fifth, *connect*. Remember to say, "I would like for you to look at me."

Sixth, *satiate*. Remember to say, "I am so pleased with this opportunity."

Then, make your statement the RILEE Karate-dō way. It is time for you to exhibit black belt mastery. So, let's see you do it.

◼ RILEE Karate Game

You are now ready to prove yourself worthy of the RILEE karate black belt. You can exhibit mastery in this game. But before you begin, remember to relax the RILEE way. Remember to breathe deeply and say to yourself, "I can feel comfy and safe, any time, any place." Now you are ready to begin,

Directions: Color six paper strips black and use them as belts. Twelve new scenarios are included here. Everyone gets to respond to each situation as a true black belt master. Everyone's a black belt bear.

Black Belt Bear

Roll the die to see who goes first. When you choose your card, remember to talk about a similar situation that happened to you. Remember to behave like a black belt as you act out your responses to the situation on the card.

RILEE Karate Situation Cards

(color me black) You are very stressed because you have overdone it.	(color me black) Your father got fired from his job.
(color me black) Someone is trying to force you to do something wrong.	(color me black) Your grandmother dropped a bag of groceries on the floor and the milk spilled.
(color me black) Your brother is teasing you about a very painful experience in your past.	(color me black) You did not make the soccer team.
(color me black) Your sister is telling everyone about the test you failed.	(color me black) Someone slapped you.
(color me black) Your father is feeling very, very sad.	(color me black) Your mother wanted a new house that the family could not afford.
(color me black) Someone lied to you.	(color me black) You were told that you couldn't go to the game.

Include the following behaviors I your responses.

* Formal behavior

* Best effort

* Serenity

* Strong character

You can kick, punch, or shout, too. But you must display a commanding, masterful presence. You may include any of the six karate-dō behaviors: relax, relate, forgive, share, connect, and satiate. You can also guide others in their efforts at black belt mastery, *if* they ask for your assistance.

You can do or say anything that displays a commanding masterful presence based on wise choices. For this is the RILEE Karate-dō black belt way of *being heard, not hurt*.

Now that you have become a black belt master at controlling your anger, it is time to learn alternatives to anger. Yes, it is possible to choose not to continue feeling angry. There are alternatives. Good relating will allow you to resolve your anger. Learn how in chapter 10.

chapter 10

Alternatives to Anger

This chapter focuses specifically on alternatives to anger and helps you recognize the beginning of your anger, so you can do something about it then, before you blow your top. You will be using information you've already learned and putting it all together to come up with a basic style of behaving. This RILEE way of relating to others, which is the focus of the workbook, will improve your relationships within your family—and with those outside of your family. When you do get angry, as everyone does, you will also have tools to help you get back on the RILEE path.

The first part of this chapter is for parents only; then we'll discuss anger alternatives for parents and children. Let's begin with the following exercise.

Exercise 10.1 What Makes You Angry?

Take some time to think about the last time you got angry. What happened? Briefly describe the situation below.

_____

_____

_____

_____

What did you do? How did you respond to your anger?

_____

_____

_____

What was the outcome? What happened after you responded to your anger?

_____

_____

_____

If the situation ended badly, the alternatives in this chapter will help you. You will refer back to this exercise later to come up with alternatives to what you did. You'll notice that some of what we will discuss sounds like common sense, and it is! As we discussed earlier, recognizing your body's response to events will help you appropriately label your feelings and notice when you feel the stirrings of anger. Then what? What do you do next?

Parenting Issues

Before we get to alternatives to anger, let's review some key concepts necessary for good parenting—and good relating.

Show Empathy

You've learned about the importance of teaching empathy to your children and using empathy in getting along better with others. Empathy may be used as a tool to help you develop awareness of your own feelings as well (Watson, Goldman, and Vanaerschot 1998). When a therapist uses empathy in relationship with a client, the therapist is also modeling, and this leads to a stronger sense of self for the client. When you, as parents, model empathy for your children, you essentially do the same thing—you are teaching your child that he or she is important! This creates a new self-confidence and helps your child recognize all of the feelings experienced, including anger. The ability to put yourself in someone else's shoes helps you recognize your own feelings.

Exercise Attachment Parenting

Sears, Sears, and Pantley (2002) discuss how anger can override empathy. But first, what is attachment parenting? Attachment parenting is a way of getting to know your child; it makes discipline easier; and it's based on mutual trust. Attachment parenting is about *strengthening relationships*, beginning in infancy. When you are angry, using your empathic skills is very difficult! You must first get control of your anger before you are able to use empathy effectively. But guess what? When you are consistently using the RILEE skills you are learning in this workbook, it gets easier and easier! The more empathic you already are, the easier it will be for you to step back from your anger and address the needs of your child.

Deal with Your Child's Anger

How do you use attachment parenting to deal with your child's anger when your child's behavior invites you to be angry? You first recognize what is affecting you. Is it that your child embarrassed you in a public place? Did your child disrespect you by calling you a name or talking back? This is when you need to step back and analyze your thoughts—and what's behind them! Is an old family affective theme emerging? Look at your child. What is motivating your child's behavior? Try to focus on the needs of your child and not on how the situation is affecting you at the moment. The latter can be addressed after you both are calm again.

Use Your Wise Voice

Once you figure out what may be motivating the actions of your child, deal with that specific thing. You may not be sure what it is, but you can probably make a pretty good guess. Talk it through with your child. Use a soft, but firm tone of voice. Use your *wise voice*. Use eye contact. Look at your child and allow your body to take a listening stance. As your child reads your body language and learns that a battle is not about to occur, she or he will be more willing to talk to you in a calm, wise voice, as well. Remember your child can choose the wise voice instead of the wild or weak voices, but you may have to initiate the process. After the crisis has passed, the two of you may then discuss your child's behavior, and if necessary, you can apply consequences.

Stay Calm

The decision to apply consequences is very important! Do you realize that not every bad behavior has to be addressed? There are times when you have to choose your battles. Certainly, if you have been working with your child on a specific behavior, then by all means, you must apply consequences immediately and consistently when your child misbehaves in that way. Even when you apply consequences, however, be mindful of what you are doing. Stay calm. Discipline is much more effective when you, the parents, are calm and aware. What does *being aware* mean? In this case, it means recognizing what's happening with your child—the very core of attachment parenting. It means being involved and looking beyond the specific acts to what may be motivating the behavior. It means looking behind the anger your child may be showing you and helping your child acknowledge the feelings inside.

The following story illustrates attachment parenting.

Elizabeth's Story

Four-year-old Elizabeth reached for the mustard and spilled her drink. The family was on the way to an appointment, and time was limited. Cleaning up Elizabeth's mess was inconvenient. Elizabeth realized that and began crying. Katie, Elizabeth's mother, got down to Elizabeth's eye level and asked, "Would you like me to help you clean it up?" Elizabeth shook her head yes, and peace was restored.

In the example above, which is similar to one cited in Sears, Sears, and Pantley (2002), simply understanding what Elizabeth needed at that time was the key to successfully dealing with what could have been a crisis. Elizabeth learned that making mistakes is okay, and she could count on her mother to assist her when she needed it.

Exercise 10.2 Attachment Parenting

Now respond to the following two scenarios with your own illustrations of attachment parenting:

1. Your four-year-old child stayed up past his bedtime, and he had not had a nap. When you tell him to get ready for bed, he says emphatically, "No!" What do you do?

_____

_____

_____

2. Your pre-teen wants to go to a PG-13 movie with friends. What do you do?

_____

_____

_____

You'll notice that there are no "right" answers to these questions. Consider the first scenario. You might choose to pick up your four-year-old and hold him close, telling him that you love him. Recognizing that he is tired and has difficulty with his regular routine will help you be more patient. You may have to assist him with changing into his pajamas and brushing his teeth, continually talking softly to him and encouraging him.

The second scenario might require negotiation. You might wish to discuss the movie at length or research it on your own before deciding. You might compromise by attending the movie with your pre-teen, with the understanding that he or she will leave immediately if the content is inappropriate.

Discipline Principles

Discipline is "giving your children the tools to succeed in life" (Sears, Sears, and Pantley 2002, 36). This concept is closely entwined with attachment parenting. Remember, attachment parenting is about strengthening relationships.

Strengthening relationships begins during infancy—connecting with your child physically and emotionally. If you and your child are to make wise choices, mutual respect must be at the base of your relationship. You must never use your child's vulnerabilities against him or her. The way you discipline your children will affect how they see anger—and how they express it.

How to Use Time-outs

One very effective way of managing misbehavior with children is to use *time-outs*. Often, however, time-outs are used ineffectively, and parents give up. Remember that time out is a behavior stopper, not a behavior starter (Clark 1996). For time-outs to be an effective tool, Clark points out, you target a specific behavior to change. For example, your child may be leaving dirty dishes in his bedroom, leaving wet towels on the floor, and throwing a temper tantrum when he does not get his way. Though these are all behaviors you may want to stop, choose one at a time as a target behavior.

Clark also stresses the importance of being clear and consistent in your use of time-outs, and suggests the following strategy:

1. Target a specific behavior.

2. Count how often this behavior occurs.

3. Choose a boring place for time-out.

4. Explain to your child that he or she will be put in time-out if the behavior occurs again.

5. Wait patiently for the targeted behavior to occur.

6. If the behavior does occur, put your child in the time-out place, using no more than ten words and ten seconds to accomplish this.

7. Get the portable timer, set it to ring in _____ minutes (one minute per age of your child), and place it within hearing distance of your child.

8. Wait for the timer to ring. Remove all attention from your child while he or she waits for the timer to ring.

9. Ask your child, after the timer rings, why he or she was sent to time-out.

After your child has successfully changed this first behavior, you may address any additional behaviors. Remember to address one behavior at a time.

Common Sense Parenting

In terms of discipline, *common sense parenting* includes making choices, being clear, employing consequences, communicating, and being consistent (Murphy and Oberlin 2002).

Make Choices

You first must decide what you will address with your children. Regarding discipline, you can't effectively deal with everything your child does. Addressing those behaviors that most annoy you makes sense. You must choose your battles!

Be Clear

Once you decide which behaviors you will address, the next step is to make sure your child knows how to change the behavior. This may require a little investigation on your part to make sure you understand the conditions under which your child misbehaves. For example, does your child behave in a certain way when she or he is tired? Is it in the morning when she or he is rushing to school or at night when she or he is struggling to complete homework? You must know your child. Understand, however, that sometimes you may not know why your child is doing something. There may not be a reason.

Employ Consequences

What ever happens after your child misbehaves, it should, ideally, be a learning experience. Consequences should be handled according to the age or developmental stage of your child. For example, for very young children, praise will work wonders, though using time-outs in addition to praise will often be necessary.

Remember to Communicate

Whatever discipline method you try with your child, you must discuss it with him or her. Children need to understand what the expectations, rules, and consequences are—before they break them! Discussing a particular problematic behavior with your child's teacher may also be necessary to ensure that you are both working toward the same end in altering the same behavior.

Be Consistent

Discipline is an ongoing process that requires constant attention. Discussing progress with other caregivers and teachers will help you remain consistent. If your child's behavior is not improving, and you are not consistent in your responses to your child's misbehavior, you cannot hold your child accountable. You are also responsible.

Alternatives to Anger (For Parents and Children)

Now that you have learned and reviewed discipline methods, focus on alternatives to anger with the rest of the family. Remember, the goal is to first identify angry feelings. Then, use alternatives.

Remember to Relax

In the last few chapters you learned to use RILEE relaxation, where you say, either aloud or silently, "I can be comfy and safe any time, any place." The more you work on helping your body—and ultimately yourself—relax, the better you will become at relaxing. After a while, exercises won't be necessary, and simply telling yourself, "I can be comfy and safe, any time, any place," will be enough to get you relaxed and back in control so that you can make better choices. Practice relaxing the RILEE way again, using everything you've learned thus far.

Exercise 10.3 RILEE Relaxation

Directions: Parents, read the following exercise aloud while your children lie comfortably with room to move. Let them act out what the exercise tells them. Of course, this exercise is not just for your children. It will help you relax, too.

Here I am
Back again
I'm RILEE, the
Re-lax-a-tion Bear
Here to remind you
Of all you learned
so that you can
Use alternatives to anger.

You can do it.
You can choose wisely.
You can choose a
Strong, strong, strong
voice.
You can choose a
clear, clear, clear
message.
You can choose a
Firm, firm, firm
tone.
You can choose to
be heard, heard, heard,
But respectfully.

So, wrinkle your nose,
Wiggle your toes,
Put a smile on you lips
and a Twinkle in your eye.
Drop your jaw, relax,
and say,

"I can be comfy and safe,
any time, any place."

Good. You can do it!
Remember to use
The "I" voice—the "wise" voice—
when you wish to
Be heard.
Remember to take a
deep, deep breath.
Remember to
Relax, relax, relax.

The RILEE
Way, way, way.
Remember to tighten

All, all, all of your muscles
From your face, face, face
down to your
Toes, toes, toes.
Now breathe, breathe, breathe,
Tighten, tighten, tighten,
Hold, hold, hold.
Now, loosen, loosen, loosen,
Let your breath go, go, go.
Good, good, good.

Now say to yourself,

"I can feel comfy and safe,
any time, any place."

Yes, you can.
You can feel comfy and safe
any time, any place.
For when you breathe deeply
and relax all of your muscles,
when you say,
"I can feel comfy and safe
any time any place,"
you will be ready to
cope with your feelings.

You can do it.
You can make the wise RILEE choices.
You can choose the "I" voice.
You can find a RILEE way,
not an angry way,
For you are a black belt master like me.

So, wrinkle your nose,
Wiggle your toes,
Put a smile on your lips,
and a twinkle in your eye.
Drop your jaw
and be a RILEE relaxation
black belt master, just like me.

Now you are truly prepared to
Find alternatives to anger,
For you are a RILEE master.
Congratulations!

How does this RILEE relaxation exercise fit in with alternatives to anger? Simply. When something happens and you feel angry, first relax. You'll notice that feeling angry is difficult when you are relaxed. When you are relaxed, you'll be more prepared to consider whether any action is necessary. You may need to use your wise voice. You may need to consider whether the wanter bear or challenger bear part of you is taking over—and stop those nasty bears.

There may be times, however, when no action is necessary. You may feel angry initially, but after you relax, realize that you were just feeling overly sensitive. Or, you may realize that any action on your part is unnecessary or could even make matters worse. You must choose your battles!

Choose Your Battles

This relates back to the idea of *choice*. You cannot address every bad behavior or every injustice done to you. There are times when some things are better left ignored. Parents, this goes for discipline. Children, there are times when it is better just to let your toddler brother or sister play with your toy until she or he grows tired of it. There are times when you don't have to respond or do anything if someone calls you a name. Sometimes, doing nothing is much more than doing something. Practice choosing your battles in the following exercise. Again, you may wish to copy the page or use a blank sheet of paper so that every family member may participate.

Exercise 10.4 Choose Your Battles

Write down the last time something happened that made you feel angry.

_____

_____

_____

_____

Think about what you did. What do you think would have happened if you had done nothing?

_____

_____

_____

_____

Remember, there are times when you can choose your battles. You can decide what needs your attention versus what does not. It's your choice.

Use Code Words

The use of *code words* or *cuing* (a mutually agreed upon word or phrase that will remind another person of the consequence of a behavior) can greatly help decrease consequences for misbehaviors. For example, saying "Remember RILEE," may help your child calm down. If someone cues you, it can help you remain in control of your behavior. Parents, you must remember that this goes for everyone. Your children can "cue" you as well!

Use Time-out and Rain Checks

When you use time-out as part of discipline, everyone is aware of the consequences, and giving consequences gets easier and easier—and less and less frequent. Taking a *rain check* can also help open the lines of communication within the family and foster trust. Sometimes it's a good idea to agree to deal with an issue later, but follow-through is essential.

Use Mommy, Daddy, and Kiddie Time

Likewise, using Mommy, Daddy, and Kiddie Time (taking a short break from the family to calm down or rest) helps you stay at your best. Parents, when you are tired, you may need to wind down after that long day at work before giving your full attention to your toddler. Understand, however, that choice of timing is crucial. If you have been away from home all day, your children probably expect to spend speical time with Mommy or Daddy right after you get home. Attend to them first—give them attention, hugs, love. Once they are satisfied and migrate back to their previous activity, then you can have a break. You may also want to use the commute home as your break. Be resourceful and respectful of all family members. If your significant other has been home all day with your small children, give him or her a break. If one of you has had a particularly difficult day at work, do the same. Remember, you are both working toward the same thing, a loving relationship for everyone.

Review

In closing, the concepts we stressed in this chapter include the use of empathy, attachment parenting, time-out, and the principles of common sense parenting. We also covered several alternatives to anger, including a RILEE relaxation exercise, choosing your battles, using code words or cues, using time-outs and rain checks, and using Mommy, Daddy, and Kiddie time. Using these techniques will not only help you improve the way you cope with your own anger, but will also improve your child's ability to deal with his or her own anger and frustration.

Remember the first exercise in this chapter? Review your responses. With that experience in mind, complete the following exercise. You may wish to copy this page or use a blank sheet of paper so that every family member may participate.

Exercise 10.5 Using the FACTS Concept

Think about the last time you got angry. Considering the alternatives you just learned, write down how you would respond to the same situation if it happened again. Write down the FACTS below.

Feeling _____

Acting _____

Thinking _____

Sensing _____

Choosing _____

Did you change anything? Were you able to use new information to help resolve a question you had before? Some of the concepts explained in this chapter may be easier to use than others, which take practice. That's okay. This is a family exercise. Just remember to relate in love every evening.

chapter 11

Family Dialogue

We've discussed several alternatives to anger. Another alternative is *family dialogue*. This is a very important RILEE way of relating. This chapter is written for parents. Use these techniques with your family.

Active Listening

Remember in chapter 1, we talked about the importance of active listening. Active listening involves four components: *listening*, *summarizing*, *restating*, and *responding*. You may not need to go through every component for each conversation, but recognizing potential breakdowns in communication is invaluable, especially when dealing with small children. When you are trying to convey an important message, asking your child to repeat what she or he heard will let you know whether the message was received. This also lets your child know that what both of you say is important, and it models interactions with other authority figures.

Good Communication

Communication involves words, body language, understanding, and listening (Sears, Sears, and Pantley 2002). Children and adults with good communication skills are more likely to be successful than those without. Think about it. Being able to discuss problems with friends will help your child have better peer relationships. Being able to communicate adequately will later help with job interviews, employee relationships, romantic relationships, and so on. These skills are necessary! Sears, Sears and Pantley (2002) point out what good communicators have in common.

* They listen attentively.

* They listen empathically.

* They think before they speak.

* They communicate with body language.

* They speak appropriately and tactfully.

* They practice self-control so that their tongues don't get them into trouble.

Each of the items included in the above list has been discussed to some degree throughout this workbook. A golden rule also applies to communication: Talk to your children the way you want them to talk to you.

Mutual Respect

Sometimes communicating is only relaying information. Often, however, your goal is to relate to someone else. Remember, relating is an interactive experience, even between you and your child. In order to relate to someone else in a positive way, mutual respect must be present. Remember, you learned that *mutual respect* is being courteous or polite to each other. As a parent, you expect respect from your children, but you also need to give respect. You are teaching your child the important lessons of daily life, including how to interact with others. If you do not give respect, how can children learn this behavior? Model respect.

Open-ended Questions

Just as you must model respect, you also model communication skills. One of the simplest ways to improve your communication with your child (or anyone, for that matter) is to ask a good question. Many times, your questions are *closed* and allow for one-word responses, which do not relay much information. Modify your question so that it is *open* and forces a multiple-word response. For example, instead of asking your child, "Did you have a good day at school today?" say, "Tell me what you did at school today." Sometimes, children may still respond with a very short reply. That's okay. Follow up the question with a more specific response (e.g., "What games did you play?"). The following exercise allows you to practice this concept.

Exercise 11.1 Open-Ended Questions

Read each closed question and rewrite it as an open-ended question.

1. Did you have a good lunch at school today?

_____

2. Did you have fun at the birthday party?

_____

3. Did you like the movie?

Modeling Communication Skills

Other tips for modeling communication skills from Sears, Sears, and Pantley (2002) are outlined below:

Narrate Your Living

To improve your child's verbal skills early on, you were probably told to talk continuously through your activities—changing diapers, giving baths, and so on. As your children grow, however, they continue to get something out of your running commentary. They enjoy being with you, talking to you.

Keep It Simple and Make It Fun

You may notice that your child has a glazed look, which quickly lets you know that your child is not hearing anything you say. Change the tone of your voice or make a funny face while you talk, depending, of course, on the message you want to give. Remember to use the developmental level of your child as your guide. Very young children love rhymes and animated facial expressions. Even older children get a giggle out of funny faces. Keep your message short, and make it interesting for your child.

Don't Worry about Speaking Correctly

Speaking comfortably is more important than speaking correctly. Teach your child that communicating is fun. Encourage your child to talk to you naturally. Your child will learn tact and politeness by example. When your child speaks to you, speak "adult talk" back, using correct grammar, but don't correct his or her grammar. Your child will correct mistakes as he or she learns more in school and will have an advantage of hearing correct grammar at home.

Study Your Child

Notice your child's way of communicating. Personal differences in the way you communicate exist. Notice these and work with your child on developing his or her speaking skills. For example, your child may use "uh" excessively (or the phrase "you know") or speak with a younger vocabulary. Don't point out mistakes, but illustrate better speech by example.

Address Your Child by Name

Model using people's names in conversations. This lets the person know you are speaking directly to him or her and stresses the importance of the other person. Speak directly to your children in conversation. Remember to ask someone's name if you were not introduced or forgot it. Being open about getting someone's name is more honest than not using a name because you forgot it. This will serve as an example for your child.

Practice Give-and-Take

Children need to have a safe environment for testing their opinions and standing up for what they believe. This does not mean that children dictate what happens in the family or that you must allow them to do what they want all the time. Practice speaking desires and opinions in the family. Provide your child with help regarding tone and word choices. Remind him or her to use a wise voice.

Monitor Communicators Outside the Family

Remember that you are not the only one modeling communication skills. Notice the messages your child receives from peers, teachers, coaches, etc. Promote relationships with others who will reinforce what you are teaching at home.

Discuss Undesirable Language

When your child says things that are not permissible, as she or he inevitably will, address it. Use a "we" message, which implies that the behavior is non-negotiable and is a family norm. For example, "We don't hit people." Another way of dealing with undesirable language is to turn the experience into an instructive moment. For example, if you and your child are in line at the grocery store and overhear young adults ahead of you using curse words, discuss this with your child. Ask your child how hearing those words affects him or her. Use the opportunity to let your child know that the language is offensive.

Respect Each Other in Dialogue

To further assist you with better communication in your family, you may consider constructing a *dialogue guide* (Gordon and Gordon 2002). Though the dialogue guide concept has been used mainly with couples, it may be modified within the whole family. A dialogue guide is a pictorial representation including several sentence stems for your use. For example, "I hope. . . ," "I notice (behavior). . . ," "I am frustrated. . . . ," and "I want (specific requests) . . ." may begin conversations with your child. When your children hear you using this language within your family, they will learn to use it outside of your family. Respecting each other while giving your opinion is at the heart of communication.

Figure 11.1 provides an example.

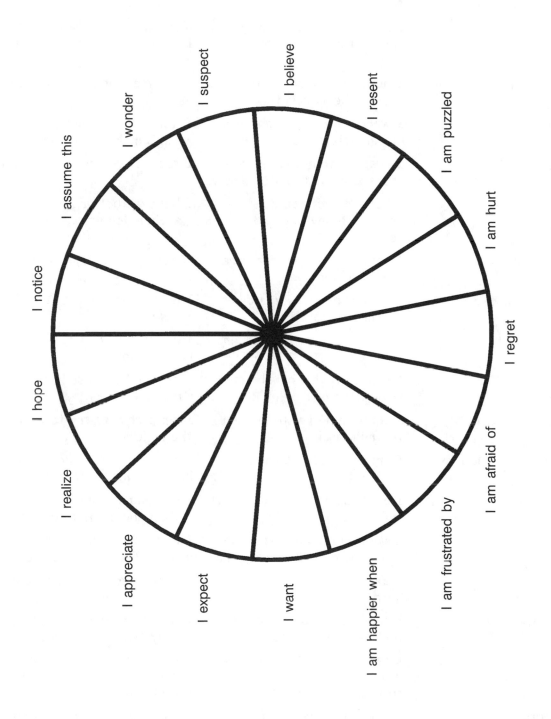

Figure 11.1 Dialogue Guide (Gordon and Gordon 2002)

There are seventeen spokes on the Gordon and Gordon dialgue guide. Here are some examples of how to use those in communicating. Remember that each family may not have to use all seventeen pieces of the guide. Feel free to construct a dialogue guide to fit your family.

"I" Statements	Mom	Johnny
"I notice"	Johnny, I noticed that you spilled the milk again.	Mom, when I spilled the milk, I notice that you yelled at me.
"I assume this means"	I assume this means that you are not being careful.	I assume this means you don't like me.
"I wonder"	I wonder why you don't pay closer attention.	I wonder why you yell at me when I make a mistake.
"I suspect"	I suspect that you get distracted by your sister, Mary.	I suspect you are very tired.
"I believe"	I believe that you don't appreciate my buying the milk for you.	I believe that you don't love me when you yell at me.
"I resent"	I resent when you are careless with the food.	I resent that it is so easy for you to yell at me.
"I am puzzled"	I am puzzled why you don't correct the problem.	I am puzzled why I can't please you.
"I am hurt"	I am hurt that this happens so much.	I am hurt when you yell at me so loudly.
"I regret"	I regret that I bought such a large container of milk.	I regret that I spilled the milk.
"I am afraid of"	I am afraid of your spilling the milk again.	I am afraid to try to pour the milk now.
"I am frustrated by"	I am frustrated by these accidents.	I am frustrated that it is so hard for me to pour the milk.
"I am happier when"	I am happier when you get it right.	I am happier when you buy milk in quarts, not gallons.
"I want"	I want you to pay attention when you are pouring the milk.	I want you to buy milk in quarts. They are a lot lighter.
"I expect"	I expect that this will be hard for you.	I expect you to buy gallons to save money.
"I appreciate"	I appreciate your giving this task your best effort.	I would appreciate your saving my feelings instead.
"I realize"	I realize that it is hard for you to pour the milk out of this large container.	I realize that this might cost a little more, so I am willing to help out.
"I hope"	I hope that you can find a way not to spill the milk in the future.	I hope you will consider my feelings and request.

More RILEE Theory

As we mentioned in chapter 2, Hendrix (1988, 1992) believes that developmental problems can influence the people we become. A clinging child fears abandonment and becomes a "clinger." A detached child fears rejection and becomes an "avoider." A distancing child fears absorption and becomes an "isolator," while an ambivalent child fears loss and becomes a "pursuer." A rigid child afraid of being shamed becomes a "controller," and an invisible child afraid of being a self becomes a "diffuser." The competitive child fears failure and becomes a "competitor." The helpless/manipulative child fears aggressiveness/success and becomes the "manipulator/compromiser." The lonely child afraid of others/ostracism becomes a "loner," while the gregarious child afraid of neediness/ being alone becomes a "caretaker." Finally, the rebellious child fears being controlled and becomes a "rebel," while the model child fears being different and becomes a "conformist."

Two people who have been developmentally blocked or traumatized growing up tend to *couple* later on in life. Clingers usually couple with avoiders; pursuers with isolators; controllers with diffusers; competitors with manipulators; caretakers with loners; and rebels with conformists. When children of these couples overhear arguments or negative *dialogue* between their parents, those children may develop prominent family affective themes that interfere with their ability to relate effectively with others.

This may be alleviated through exercising the different RILEE needs you learned earlier: secure attachment, attention, acceptance, approval, acknowledgement, and affection. When clinger/avoider couples produce scared children, secure attachment will comfort the children. Likewise, pursuer/isolator couples produce angry children, who feel friendly after getting necessary attention. Anxious children of controller/diffuser couples feel calm after receiving acceptance, and embarrassed children of competitor/manipulator couples feel proud when given approval. Caretaker/loner couples produce sad children, who become glad with acknowledgment, and rebel/conformist couples produce unrealistically happy children, who learn to balance gloomy and happy feelings after receiving permission to feel all feelings via unconditional affection.

The following examples of dialogue show how this works:

Clinger: I noticed that you went to the movies without me.

Avoider: I want to go to the movies sometimes just with my friends.

Clinger: I am happier when we spend a lot of time together.

Avoider: I resent it when I don't have space.

Clinger: I hope that you will make special time to be with me.

Avoider: I am frustrated when I don't get "alone" time.

Clinger: I am frustrated by your wandering off.

Avoider: I am wondering why you are so suspicious.

Clinger: I assume this means you don't want me around.

Avoider: I appreciate it when you trust me more.

When your children overhear this dialogue (yes, they do listen), they become very scared. It is difficult for them to attach to you when you are having difficulty attaching to each other. When you can dialogue more successfully, they can experience more comfort.

Pursuer: I noticed that you are gone every morning when I wake up.

Isolator: I like to go jogging first thing in the morning.

Pursuer: I want you to cuddle with me before you get out of bed in the mornings.

Isolator: I have a busy schedule.

Pursuer: I am frustrated that when I want to go to lunch, you're too busy.

Isolator: I just need some space.

Isolator: I want you to go out with your friends.

Pursuer: Then you might go out and wouldn't be home when I got back.

Pursuer: I appreciate it if you would give this a chance.

Isolator: Stop asking me for this.

When your children overhear this dialogue, they become very angry. It is difficult for them to arrange for you to give them positive attention when you are having difficulty giving each other positive attention. When you can dialogue more successfully, they can experience a friendlier home environment.

Controller: I am frustrated that you don't seem to know what you want.

Diffuser: I don't know what I want, but I don't want you to tell me that.

Controller: I regret sometimes that I even bother with you.

Diffuser: I will do better next time.

Controller: I assume this means you are resisting my authority.

Diffuser: No, you are right. I just want you to see my point.

Controller: I suspect that if you would get up earlier, you would be on time for things.

Diffuser: You don't notice all the things I do every morning.

Controller: I am happier when you do just as I say.

Diffuser: You don't even care about my happiness.

When your children overhear this dialogue, they become very anxious. It is difficult for them to feel accepted when you are having difficulty accepting each other. When you can dialogue more successfully, they can experience a calmer home environment.

Competitor: I noticed that you didn't even try to win the piano competition.

Manipulator: I was just playing because I like to.

Competitor: I wonder why you can't do anything right.

Manipulator: I'm doing the best I can.

Competitor: I am frustrated that you sat by yourself at the party.

Manipulator: You weren't paying any attention to me.

Competitor: I expected you to hit that ball—it went right by you.

Manipulator: Can't you just play for fun?

Competitor: I regret that you didn't listen to me—you'd have gotten that promotion.

Manipulator: I like the job I'm in now.

When your children overhear this dialogue, they become very embarrassed. It is difficult for them to feel your approval when you are having such difficulty approving of one another. When you can dialogue more successfully, they can feel proud.

Caretaker: I hope Molly and Jake can come over for dinner.

Loner: I'd really rather not have company tonight.

Caretaker: I want to know what's bothering you.

Loner: I don't have to tell you everything that I'm thinking.

Caretaker: I wonder why you don't get out more.

Loner: I prefer to stay at home and read.

Caretaker: I hope you'll come to the party at my office.

Loner: I doubt I'll go.

Caretaker: I expect you to let me know what I can do for you to make you feel better.

Loner: Sometimes I don't want you to do anything.

When your children overhear this dialogue, they become very sad. It is difficult for them to acknowledge when you are having difficulty acknowledging one another. When you can dialogue more successfully, they can experience more gladness.

Rebel: I notice that you don't like my tattoo.

Conformist: I don't mind it—just so you keep it covered when we go out in public.

Rebel: I want you to go to that new club with me.

Conformist: I can't go there because someone from work might see me.

Rebel: I expect you to side with me in arguments.

Conformist: I was just trying to be nice.

Rebel: I wonder why you won't get a tattoo.

Conformist: I would only get one that I can cover up for work.

Rebel: I hope you tell them that you did the same thing.

Conformist: I will only if they seem to agree with it.

When your children overhear this dialogue, they become superficially happy. It is difficult for them to be affectionate toward you when you are having difficulty being affectionate toward each other. When you can dialogue more successfully, they can experience more genuine feelings.

As you can see, if you are engaged in this type of pairing, using the dialogue wheel technique without remembering the "I" statements and wise voice won't work. In order to make it work, you must first break the dynamic of the trait couple interactions. You must get rid of the FATs! One way of doing this is to use active listening. The following suggestions may help you do this.

Listen completely and attentively. Don't think. Don't prepare your rebuttal. Don't interrupt.

Summarize what you heard the other person say. Don't interpret. Don't go beyond what was said.

Clarify before you respond. Give the other person an opportunity to correct any misinterpretations (yours or someone else's).

Restate your summary. Understand what the other person is thinking. Follow the person's logic. Understand how the person came to that conclusion.

Empathize with the other person's feelings. Don't focus on your feelings. Remember, you can empathize without agreeing.

Respond. Don't react. Consider the other person's position. Seek compromise. Don't judge; rather, relate.

In conclusion, you can either be right or be related, not both. When you try to be right, you are stuck in your FATs. Be related; live in your FACTS. You may notice initially that you are the one making the "compromises." Don't give up—you're modeling appropriate behavior and good communication skills for your significant other and your child. Remember, the goal is relating. When you are using the dialogue guide, "I" statements, and a wise voice, combined with active listening, you are on your way to *relating in love every evening.*

When you master good choices, your family prospers. Your children will feel comfy and friendly. They will learn to calm themselves in difficult situations and feel proud of their accomplishments—even when they occasionally make mistakes. Their general dispositions will be glad, and they will be free to feel gloomy when appropriate.

chapter 12

Making Good Choices

Thank you for joining us on the RILEE path to loving family relatedness. As you have learned in the preceding chapters, relating in love every evening is a very ordinary process, but with very extraordinary results. It is about creating joy rather than pain, hope rather than despair, and kindness rather than cruelty. Your children are your most precious gifts. They must be nurtured, guided, equipped, and protected throughout the development process so that they can grow without being traumatized.

Many believe that parenting is an automatic process, something that just happens. Wouldn't it be wonderful if that were true? Perhaps centuries ago, when family life was less complicated, it might have been true. But in today's very complex world, the need to nurture, guide, equip, and protect children is more necessary than ever. Parenting is not an automatic process. So, helping your children to make good choices begins with you.

Good Parenting: Be Prepared

In the first part of this workbook, you were asked to adopt a new perspective. Understanding how children learn and relate is powerful information. It will help you to create a safer emotional environment for your family. Many adults perceive parenting to be about being in control. Yet being in control at all times under all circumstances is impossible. When it is possible, it is fleeting. External controls last only so long.

Good parenting is about building a relationship with your children. When you offer your children the six RILEE A's—attachment security, attention, acceptance, approval, acknowledgement, and affection—and when you actively listen to their concerns, they will do so in return. By creating a family atmosphere of mutual respect, you are arranging for your children to thrive. Everyone will then be on the RILEE path. It's a matter of choice.

The First Choice: Believe That You Can Change

In order for you to create a safe environment for your children and to proceed down the RILEE path, you must first address your own developmental wounds. It would be wonderful if you didn't have any, but childhood's aren't perfect. It is important for you to believe that you can resolve your own childhood "traumas." This must be your first choice. Without choosing to face and resolve your own childhood traumas, you cannot be a good parent. Good parenting begins with you. Telling a child to do as you say and not as you do is ineffective, for children learn first and foremost through imitation. Double binding a child to do it—but to do it your way—is also ineffective. Children learn through experience. Children must have the opportunity to try things, to explore, to make mistakes, and to be loved unconditionally.

Loving a child unconditionally does not, however, mean abdicating your disciplinary responsibilities. Rather, it means creating discipline by example. Giving children clear, single-command messages, citing consequences, and offering alternatives is a very powerful form of parenting. Children will learn through your good example. It is such a joy to see young children follow the lead of their parents and carefully show other children how to complete a task successfully.

The Second Choice: Let Go of the Past

More than likely you began your parenting journey with lots of old baggage, baggage that was chosen for you. Most, if not all, childhood traumas were thrust upon us. Seldom do we arrange such difficulties for ourselves. Yet we must carry the burden of these difficulties ourselves. This is what baggage is all about. Baggage is a burden. Life is too full of present problems. Carrying ever-present problems from the past is too much of a burden. Therefore, you must turn your old baggage into luggage. Why luggage? Luggage has wheels and handles. It is streamlined. It can hold only so much. There is no room for burdens, only for memories. It is okay to pack your memories into your luggage, for you need perspective. It is not okay to pack your old trait emotions, however. They take up too much room, for they are filled with FATs.

In order for you to be an effective parent, you must understand your family affective themes and choose to not inflict them on your children. It is your responsibility to resolve your FATs traumas.

The Third Choice: Adopt a Parenting Style Based on Self-Discipline.

Adopting a new lifestyle that requires ongoing choices is never easy. It takes a lot of discipline. But how can you effectively discipline yourself? Self-discipline is a choice that must be made each and every day. There is no such thing as time off for good behavior. Every day is about leading by example, relating in love, and making wise choices. You as a parent are on duty full time, and full time is more than forty hours a week. It is forever.

But this is not a burden. It is a healthy choice. Only unhealthy choices and unresolved traumas become burdens.

So, find your developmental wounds, address your pain, and leave those old trait feelings behind. You don't need them. You need to pack only the memories, not the pain.

One of the best ways to resolve any of the six developmental stage traumas is by giving and receiving the six RILEE A's—the six gifts of love. Oftentimes when you have been deeply wounded, you will not allow yourself to receive these six gifts of love. Yet emotional healing is an interactive process. Only by receiving can you give. Only by giving can you receive. And only in this process can you be healed. You may, however, perceive this to be an intellectual process. It is not. It is an emotional process filled with joy and hope and kindness. It is the process of play. Allow yourself to play with your children, for it is a very healing journey.

The Fourth Choice: Allow Yourself to Learn and Heal Through Play

Now you know why we have asked RILEE Bear to join us on this amazing journey. RILEE knows how to play. Playing is the key to relating in love every evening. Children learn through play. Adults heal through play. RILEE families are created through play. Families are bonded through playful experiences. Remember, healthy play nurtures, guides, equips, and protects your children. It gives them an opportunity to learn through imitation, experience, and example. It helps them to share their feelings, to learn how others may be feeling, and to understand different viewpoints. It also helps them to accept rules and limits. In order to be a good parent, you must be willing to play.

So, are you prepared to be a good parent? Do you believe you can change? Will you let go of the pain of the past? Will you accept the self-discipline inherent in the RILEE path? And will you choose to learn and heal through play? If your answers to these four fundamental questions are "yes," then you are in the process of preparing yourself to be a good parent. Having a healthy historical, theoretical, and emotional basis for parenting is, however, only the first part of the journey.

Good Teaching: The Next Four Steps

The next part of the journey is preparing yourself to be an effective teacher. Teaching is a very important process. It involves knowing what to teach (the content), and how to teach it (the process). Being equipped with IQ, without EQ (emotional quotient), is a disaster. Being equipped with EQ, without IQ, is equally problematic. As a parent you must know what to teach and how to teach it.

The Fifth Choice: Teach the FACTS Via Patience and Tolerance

Teaching is a very difficult job. It requires the ultimate in patience and tolerance. When you teach your children to respond rather than to react, you must have patience. You must be able to tolerate their mistakes and guide them to better choices. Because they are children, a more playful approach is needed.

Learning must be fun. Making even the most boring history lessons fun will intrigue your children. The more interactive, the more hands-on children's experiences are, the better and faster they will learn.

Two of the most enduring learning experiences come to us via traumatic events and playful events. There is enough trauma in life. We don't need to create it at home. Home is about freedom (rights times responsibilities), and freedom is about play. So, teach your children about their own emerging self by using creative play. Even the most difficult concepts can be taught using this light-hearted approach.

The Sixth Choice: Follow the Road toward Mastery

Anger is clearly a lack of mastery. When you or your children react in anger, you are merely displaying your lack of appropriate training. No RILEE karate-do master exhibits a lack of mastery. But beginners do. So, start at the beginning. Understand that mastery is a journey. It is about internal motivation and control, not external motivation and control. You have chosen to be a good parent. You have given yourself a healthy perspective. You have begun your journey. Now you must learn the information and techniques (the content and process) you need to be an effective teacher.

Understanding the stages of anger, understanding what you and your children look like when angry, understanding how RILEE's cousins can instigate anger in your family, and understanding how to make better choices are fundamental factors. Making contracts to stop teasing, blaming, wanting, and challenging can help to prevent, diffuse, contain, and resolve many family problems. Choosing the road to mastery by understanding how anger works is an important step along the journey. But remember, it involves both content and process, and it must be fun. Remember, it takes practice, patience, confidence, and strong character to be a good teacher. For that is what mastery is all about.

The Seventh Choice: Keep Your Mind and Body Calm

When was the last time you were angry? A minute ago, yesterday, last week? Do you remember how your body expressed that anger? Do you remember how it felt to be on red alert? Memorize the signs so that you can calm your body before it goes on red alert.

You can do this. You can teach yourself and your children to catch yourselves in the process—during the build-up stage. You can use deep breathing. You can say, "I can keep myself comfy and safe, any time, any place." You can recognize your anger before you react defensively, for once you react, it is all downhill. By that time a chain of events has been set in motion, often with disastrous results.

Healthy parents do not intentionally try to wound or traumatize their children. Yet they do so every day. Perhaps you do it as well. This happens every time you lose control of your anger and react defensively. Sometimes it may only be a little wound. At other times it may be a full-fledged trauma. *Remember it is not your intention but rather your child's perception that endures.* Therefore, you must choose the road toward mastery. Mastery requires a calm mind and a calm body so that you can deal with bothersome problems.

When family members wallow, intrude, think in circles, and overreact, they are creating feelings, actions, thoughts, and sensations that are very hard to handle. Teach your family to communicate, relate, listen, and behave. For these are RILEE responses rather than angry reactions. But they require an understanding of what is happening (the content) and a method for how to deal with the problem (the process). When you and your family have calm minds and calm bodies, you can look deep into your hearts for those wise RILEE choices. They will be there for you. Trust yourself and your family to choose wisely.

The Eighth Choice: Master Your Feelings and Your Actions

Once an angry reaction has taken place, as a good teacher, you must shift focus to damage control. This is about intervention. But this is an uphill solution for a downhill problem. This is a difficult and exhausting process.

The better process is prevention. Prevention involves listening, understanding, considering, problem solving, and communicating before the disaster occurs. It involves making wise choices along the way. You can master your responses to family members who are reactive, who challenge, and who tease. Those who *react* aim for your feelings. Don't allow yourself to be overwhelmed by them. Those who *challenge* aim for your thoughts. Don't allow yourself to debate with them. They want you to take them on. Don't do it. Those who *tease* aim for your actions. They want to victimize you. They want to see you dissolve into a pool of low self-esteem right in front of their very eyes. Don't allow them to victimize you.

Maintain your power! Move from red alert to brown alert. There is no such person as a red belt master. Those who choose to be red belts are hardly masters. They toy with your thoughts, your feelings, and your actions. They try to strip you of esteem. They maintain their power at your expense. Real power is never achieved at someone else's expense. Power is a personal journey. It is a journey toward self-mastery, not toward mastery of others. Self-mastering invites others to respect you, as you respect others. Self-mastery is about mutual respect. Mutual respect is the RILEE way.

So are you prepared to be a good teacher? Will you teach the FACTS via patience and tolerance? Will you choose the road toward mastery? Will you learn to calm your mind and body? Will you learn to master your feelings and actions? If your answer to these questions is "yes," then you are in the process of preparing yourself to be a good teacher. Having good information and techniques will allow you to guide your children through some of the most difficult tasks in life—the tasks of understanding how to recognize, label, and manage their feelings.

Good Relating: The Final Four Steps

Managing your feelings is about mastery. Mastery is about using polite and courteous (formal) behavior, wise decision making, and comforting feelings and sensations in order to produce your best effort. When you act with black belt mastery, you are acting the RILEE way.

The Ninth Choice: Use the Wise Voice of Relating

The RILEE way is the voice of discipline. The RILEE way is the voice of play. The RILEE way is the voice of love. When you choose RILEE behaviors, you relax, relate, forgive, share, connect, and satiate. In a RILEE atmosphere, you are enough and have enough. You can give and receive freely. You can grow and heal. You can be heard, not hurt. No more weak voice! No more wild voice! Just firm, wise RILEE choices.

It is not always easy to he heard, not hurt. Sometimes as a parent, you may feel frantic or angry or lonely. At other times you may feel troubled or inadequate. Perhaps you may want to just let yourself go and indulge in whatever will take you away from the tasks of parenting. But such behaviors block relating. And relating is what the next four steps are all about.

After you have prepared yourself to be a good parent, after you have learned enough information and technical skills to be a good teacher, there is a third step. It is the step of relating. It is the step of talking *with* your children, not *at* your children. It is a big step. It is about sharing control rather than being in control. It is about mutual respect. By the time you have reached this two-thirds point along your RILEE journey, you have come to realize that respect is given, not learned. What is earned is self-respect. And this comes from within. When you have achieved self-respect in your family, others have as well.

Remember, it is possible to have more than one black belt master per family. In fact, that is the goal—for all family members to achieve black belt mastery. It is in such a RILEE atmosphere that mutual respect is achieved.

The Tenth Choice: Find Healthy Alternatives to Anger

Healthy RILEE families relate. No one person dominates. Wise choices are not always easy choices. They require discipline, RILEE discipline. Choosing to remain attached when your children are distressed, choosing to set flexible limits when your children want to explore, choosing to remain calm when your children become frantic, choosing to remain steadfast when your children want their own way, and choosing to be tolerant when your children try to be different are all wise alternatives to anger.

Sometimes it comes down to a simple flip of a coin. Are you going to remember when you need Mommy or Daddy time instead of putting your child in time-out? Are you going to be consistent and loving in your discipline? Are you going to set reasonable goals and target only a few behaviors at a time? Are you going to manage your stress levels appropriately and encourage your family to do so as well? If you choose to do these things, then you are arranging alternatives to anger. This is what relating is all about. It is about making wise RILEE choices rather than wildly indulgent or weakly defective angry choices. What you choose is who you are. For, in the final analysis, all that counts is behavior! And at this point, your behavior is a matter of choice, not chance.

The Eleventh Choice: Become an Effective Communicator

Now that you have achieved RILEE mastery, you know that good relating is all about communication. And communication requires dialogue—RILEE dialogue. Whether you started out as a clinger or a loner, whether you were a rebel or a controller, whether you tried manipulating or caretaking, none of these positions matter at this point. For it is not who you were when you started that matters. It is who you have become along the way that matters. Remember, the process of becoming requires dialogue.

The Twelfth Choice: Parent, Teach, and Relate the RILEE Way

If at the end of this workbook you are still using your angry voice, don't despair. Practice the techniques you have learned. You have had years of practice using your angry voice. It may take you some time to develop your RILEE voice. You will succeed!. Remember that your success is the greatest gift you can give your children. Having assisted you in this wonderful RILEE journey has been a joy. But remember, the RILEE path is not a "sometimes thing," it is a lifetime commitment filled with kindness and hope and love. It is about making good choices.

Your Twelve RILEE Choices

We've summarized twelve RILEE choices in two lists (one for parents and one for children). We hope that you remember to make these choices every day. Allow them to become life-long commitments. Fill your family with kindness, hope, and love.

Twelve RILEE Choices for Parents

1. I choose to believe that I can change.

2. I choose to let go of my past.

3. I choose to adopt a parenting style based on self-discipline.

4. I choose to learn and heal through play.

5. I choose to teach the FACTS with patience and tolerance.

6. I choose to follow the road toward mastery.

7. I choose to keep my mind and body calm.

8. I choose to master my feelings and my actions.

9. I choose to use the wise voice of relating.

10. I choose to find healthy alternatives to anger.

11. I choose to become an effective communicator.

12. I choose to parent, teach, and relate the RILEE way .

Twelve RILEE Choices for Children

1. I choose to believe that I can change.

2. I choose to let go of the bad and look forward to the good.

3. I choose to learn self-discipline.

4. I choose to learn to relate through play.

5. I choose to learn the FACTS with an open mind.

6. I choose to follow the road toward mastery.

7. I choose to keep my mind and body calm.

8. I choose to master my feelings and my actions.

9. I choose to use the wise voice of relating.

10. I choose to find healthy alternatives to anger.

11. I choose to become an effective communicator.

12. I choose to relate the RILEE way.

RILEE

Relating in Love

Every Evening!

References

Bar-Levav, R. 1988. *Thinking in the Shadow of Feelings: A New Understanding of the Hidden Forces That Shape Individuals and Societies*. New York: Simon and Schuster.

Beck, J. 1995. *Cognitive Therapy: Basics and Beyond*. New York: Guilford Press.

Bowlby, J. 1969. *Attachment and Loss*, vol. 1: *Attachment*. London: Hogarth Press.

Budzynski, T. 1977. Tuning in on the twilight zone. *Psychology Today* 11(3): 38-44.

Clark, L. 1996. *SOS Help for Parents*, 2nd ed. Bowling Green, Ky.: Parents Press.

Diamond, G. S., and H. A. Liddle. 1999. Transforming negative parent adolescent interactions: From impasse to dialogue. *Family Process* 38(1): 5-26.

Dodge, K. A., R. R. Murphy, and K. Buchsbaum. 1984. The assessment of intention-cue detection skills in children: Implications for developmental psychopathology. *Child Development* 55:163-173.

Fielding, B. 1999. *The Memory Manual: 10 Simple Things You Can Do to Improve Your Memory After 50*. Clovis, Calif.: Quill Driver Books.

Gordon, L. H., and M. Gordon. 2002. As used in Sager and Brown's Workshop on Intimacy: Couples' therapy, couples' groups and psychoeducation. Dialogue Guide used by permission of the author.

Gruber, H. E., and J. J. Voneche, eds. 1977. *The Essential Piaget: An Interpretive Reference and Guide*. New York: Basic Books.

Guerin, P. J., Jr., and D. R. Chabot. 1997. Development of family systems theory. In *The History of Psychotherapy: A Century of Change*, edited by D. Freedheim. Washington, D.C.: American Psychological Association.

Hall, R. V., and M. C. Hall. 1987. The basic techniques of discipline. In *Good Behavior*, edited by S. W. Garber, M. D. Garber, and R. F. Spizman. New York: Villard Books.

Hassell, R. G., and E. Otis. 2000. *The Complete Idiot's Guide to Karate*. Indianapolis: Alpha Books.

Hendrix, H. 1992. *Keeping the Love You Find: A Guide for Singles*. New York: Simon and Schuster, Inc.

———. 1988. *Getting the Love You Want: A Guide for Couples*. New York: Harper and Row.

James, M., and D. Jongeward. 1973. *Born to Win: Transactional Analysis with Gestalt Experiments*. Menlo Park, Calif.: Addison-Wesley.

Jernberg, A. M. 1979. *Theraplay*. San Francisco: Jossey-Bass.

Luquet, W. 1996. *Short Term Couples Therapy: The Imago Model in Action*. New York: Brunner/Mazel.

Murphy, T., and L. H. Oberlin. 2001. *The Angry Child: Regaining Control When Your Child Is Out of Control*. New York: Clarkson Potter Publishers.

Rogers, C. R. 1959. A theory of therapy, personality, and interpersonal relationships, as developed in the client-centered framework. In *Psychology: A Study of Science*, vol. III, *Formulations of the Person and the Social Context* edited by S. Koch. New York: McGraw-Hill.

Sadker, M., and D. Sadker. 1994. *Failing at Fairness: How America's Schools Cheat Girls*. New York: Charles Scribner's Sons.

Scarf, M. 1995. *Intimate Worlds: Life Inside the Family*. New York: Random House.

Sears, W., M. Sears, and E. Pantley. 2002. *The Successful Child: What Parents Can Do to Help Kids Turn Out Well*. Boston: Little, Brown, and Company.

Shapiro, L. E. 1997. *How to Raise a Child with a High EQ: A Parents' Guide to Emotional Intelligence*. New York: HarperCollins.

Smith, P. K., H. Cowie, and M. Blades. 1998. *Understanding Children's Development*, 3rd ed. Malden, Mass.: Blackwell Publishers.

Speilberger, C. D. 1979. *State-Trait Anger Expression Inventory*. Odessa, Fla.: Psychological Assessment Resources, Inc.

Watson, J. C., R. Goldman, and G. Vanaerschot. 1998. Empathic: A postmodern way of being? In *Handbook of Experiential Psychotherapy*, edited by L. S. Greenberg, J. C. Watson, and G. Lietaer. New York: Guilford Press.

Wynne, L. C. 1984. The epigenesis of relational systems: A model for understanding family development. *Family Process* 23(3): 297-318.

Darlyne Gaynor Nemeth, Ph.D., is a clinical and neuropsychologist with Neuropsychology Center of Louisiana, located at The Drusilla Clinic in Baton Rouge, Louisiana. Nemeth, an APA fellow, developed the breakthrough anger-management program on which this book is based. A pioneer in the area of clinical neuropsychology for more than twenty-five years, Nemeth has focused much of her practice on children's issues.

Kelly Paulk Ray, Ph.D., has served as chief psychologist at the Louisiana State University Health Sciences Center Juvenile Corrections Assessment Center and is a counseling psychologist at The Drusilla Clinic, both in Baton Rouge, Louisiana. Ray has been instrumental in developing the parents' part of the children's anger-management program and has worked extensively with the parents of school-age children.

Maydel Morin Schexnayder, MS, CRC, is a rehabilitation counselor with Louisiana Rehabilitation Services. During her years as a clinical assistant at The Neuropsychology Center for Louisiana in Baton Rouge, she served as the primary facilitator for the children's anger-management groups.

Some Other
New Harbinger Titles

The Stepparent's Survival Guide, Item SSG $17.95

Drugs and Your Kid, Item DYK $15.95

The Daughter-In-Law's Survival Guide, Item DSG $12.95

Whose Life Is It Anyway?, Item WLAW $14.95

It Happened to Me, Item IHPM $17.95

Act it Out, Item AIO $19.95

Parenting Your Older Adopted Child, Item PYAO $16.95

Boy Talk, Item BTLK $14.95

Talking to Alzheimer's, Item TTA $12.95

Helping a Child with Nonverbal Learning Disorder or Asperger's Syndrome, Item HCNL $14.95

The 50 Best Ways to Simplify Your Life, Item FWSL $11.95

When Anger Hurts Your Relationship, Item WARY $13.95

The Couple's Survival Workbook, Item CPSU $18.95

Loving Your Teenage Daughter, Item LYTD $14.95

The Hidden Feeling of Motherhood, Item HFM $14.95

Parenting Well When You're Depressed, Item PWWY $17.95

Thinking Pregnant, Item TKPG $13.95

Pregnancy Stories, Item PS $14.95

The Co-Parenting Survival Guide, Item CPSG $14.95

Family Guide to Emotional Wellness, Item FGEW $24.95

How to Survive and Thrive in an Empty Nest, Item NEST $13.95

Children of the Self-Absorbed, Item CSAB $14.95

The Adoption Reunion Survival Guide, Item ARSG $13.95

Undefended Love, Item UNLO $13.95

Why Can't I Be the Parent I Want to Be?, Item PRNT $12.95

Kid Cooperation, Item COOP $14.95

Breathing Room: Creating Space to Be a Couple, Item BR $14.95

Why Children Misbehave and What to Do About It, Item BEHV $14.95

Call **toll free, 1-800-748-6273,** or log on to our online bookstore at **www.newharbinger.com** to order. Have your Visa or Mastercard number ready. Or send a check for the titles you want to New Harbinger Publications, Inc., 5674 Shattuck Ave., Oakland, CA 94609. Include $4.50 for the first book and 75¢ for each additional book, to cover shipping and handling. (California residents please include appropriate sales tax.) Allow two to five weeks for delivery.

Prices subject to change without notice.